The Yoga of Gita

Scriptural guidelines to success, serenity, harmony and happiness

Dr Ram Shanker Tiwari

Pustak Mahal®

Publishers
Pustak Mahal®

J-3/16 , Daryaganj, New Delhi-110002
☎ 23276539, 23272783, 23272784 • *Fax:* 011-23260518
E-mail: info@pustakmahal.com • *Website:* www.pustakmahal.com

Sales Centre

- 10-B, Netaji Subhash Marg, Daryaganj, New Delhi-110002
  ☎ 23268292, 23268293, 23279900 • *Fax:* 011-23280567
  E-mail: rapidexdelhi@indiatimes.com
- 6686, Khari Baoli, Delhi-110006
  ☎ 23944314, 23911979

Branches

Bengaluru: ☎ 080-22234025 • *Telefax:* 080-22240209
E-mail: pustak@airtelmail.in • pustak@sancharnet.in
Mumbai: ☎ 022-22010941, 022-22053387
E-mail: rapidex@bom5.vsnl.net.in
Patna: ☎ 0612-3294193 • *Telefax:* 0612-2302719
E-mail: rapidexptn@rediffmail.com
Hyderabad: *Telefax:* 040-24737290
E-mail: pustakmahalhyd@yahoo.co.in

ISBN 978-81-223-0850-3

Edition: 2011

Printed at : **Glorious Printers, Delhi**

Dedication

This book is dedicated to my maternal Grandfather and Grandmother – the Late Shri Kunji Lal Upadhyay and the Late Shrimati Jamna Bai Upadhyay, of the town Timarni, Dist. Harda, Madhya Pradesh – who brought me up and reared me right from the age of three. They educated me and also nourished me with the nectar of devotion and love of the Almighty. Both were gems of humane values and virtues, overflowing with compassion for all, and with a deep devotion to Lord Shiva. I owe my humble achievements in life and my mindset for spirituality to both of them.

The dedication of this Grace of Krishna is only a symbolic iota of my respect, reverence and love for them.

Acknowledgement

My maternal Grandfather and Grandmother sowed the seeds of spirituality in my thinking right from childhood. They were achievers in the Yoga of Devotion. Till now, such seeds, time and again, have sprouted, flowered, and fruited during my lifespan. The opportunities of listening to seekers, thinkers, sages and knowledgeables, and also a perpetual longing for studying the scriptures, sprinkled the shower of His Grace upon my being.

During several short as well as long visits to foreign countries since 1970, I have always felt that the Indians and non-Indians with whom I had several opportunities to talk about the *Bhagavad Gita* and meditation were always enthusiastic to learn more about these realms of knowledge, irrespective of their faiths, but in a cut-and-dried fashion, that is, in a simple manner, without the winding, intricate complexities of the subject. Although I am aware that the wisdom has flowed earlier from the writings of yogis, philosophers, sages and the realised ones, yet an instinctive, unknown force prompted me to put my thoughts in a manner that I understand the subject now and as I wish the young generation understands it. I am grateful to the known and unknown persons who initiated the idea as presented here.

After closing the chapter of my career of 43 years as a plant-and-earth science researcher, I began writing short stories and satires aiming at the present-day array of society. On reading these, Dr (Mrs) Archana Tripathi, one of my students and also a longstanding colleague, commented that while it is good to write on lighter aspects of life, it would be more appropriate if I wrote something serious on enduring fabrics of life. This view gave me the incentive and courage to take up this venture. I am grateful to her for the impetus to undertake such a purposeful activity.

I owe gratitude to my family members who sacrificed their quality time of my company while I was busy writing and preparing the manuscript.

To Anita and Dinesh (my daughter and son-in-law), Swati and Sanjay (my elder daughter-in-law and son), Seema and Rajesh (younger daughter-in-law and son), and Vishnu Kanta (my wife), I owe special gratitude and thanks for the unabated encouragement.

I am especially indebted to Shri Keshav Prasad Dwivedi (the father of my son-in-law), who himself is a high achiever in the knowledge of the scriptures, for his supportive enthusiasm during the progress of my efforts. To Dr MS Rawat, my intimate friend of very long standing, I owe gratitude for his constant encouragement during the progress of this work.

The brilliant contributions by various authors cited in 'Selected Reading', and also by several other wise persons are gratefully acknowledged as important sources of several concepts discussed herein.

I hope this small book will be of some use for seekers interested in the wisdom of the *Gita* and Yoga through which a prudential life can be lived. If this is taken up by readers with the right perspective to achieve the goal of their life, it will be my fulfilment.

—Dr Ram Shanker Tiwari

Preface

Srimad Bhagavad Gita is a part of *Srimad Bhagavad Puran* – a Great Epic written in Sanskrit verse by the sage-poet Vyasa. The *Puran* contains musical lyrics on episodes woven around the Eternal embodiment of Lord Krishna, the splendour of His life and teachings, besides love and devotion to the Divine, codes for blissful living and the *Dharma*, i.e., the right way of living. In the *Gita*, the essence of universal wisdom, the science of human nature, the philosophy of creation, the Ultimate Reality, and the technique to attain that Truth have been narrated by Krishna to his friend and devotee – Arjuna.

This knowledge was imparted in a tense situation, in the centre of the battlefield, just when the Mahabharata war was about to begin between the families of cousin brothers – the Kauravas and the Pandavas. Krishna was the charioteer of one of the Pandava princes, Arjuna, the chief archer, who had no desire to fight his kinsmen for the sake of regaining their kingdom, which was captured by the Kauravas through deceit. Ultimately, the divine light of the *Gita* dispels the darkness of emotional breakdown in Arjuna. He acts and he wins.

This book is a simple rendition of the main aspects given in the 18 chapters of the *Gita*. Herein, each chapter is informally divided into two portions: the first half, up to the divider mark, is based on the original concept, abridged from the *Gita*; and the second half, after the divider mark, includes a simplified interpretative comment by the author. At the end of each chapter, a ten-point *Gita Gyan* is appended, which again is the author's attempt to summarise the chapter in a simple way, while incorporating all its essential elements.

A brief account of Yoga and meditation is appended at the end; this may be useful for beginners. Also, to prompt self-search thereafter, the author has added two verses on self-reflection.

In Hinduism, Krishna is adored as an incarnation of Lord Vishnu, the Supreme who sustains Creation. Hence, Krishna has always been addressed as 'Lord Krishna', 'God Krishna', and 'Bhagwan Sri Krishna' in the epics and scriptures. Also, Krishna has been totally established in the Absolute Reality through Eternal Yoga, hence He is to be conceptualised as Supreme with total attributes of the Almighty. He is Yogiraj Krishna – the King of Yoga, Who is One with Pure Consciousness. Throughout the present work, He is referred to simply as 'Krishna' – meaning thereby 'Lord Krishna'; the informality brings simplicity and proximity. Yet, Krishna is addressed as 'He' – with a capital 'H', a symbolic connotation of His Greatness as Pure Consciousness. While talking to Arjuna, Krishna was One with the Absolute; He speaks in Direct Speech – First Person Singular, e.g., "All this world is pervaded by Me in My unmanifested form." In the text herein, however, for the sake of facile running of the statements and simplification, an Indirect Speech has been used.

While referring to human beings, the epithets 'he', 'his', 'him', etc, are used, yet they must be taken to include both male and female – again an adoption for plainness and non-repetition. So also, Godheads or even the Absolute, the Almighty are referred to as 'He', etc. This does not imply male chauvinism but is suggestive of the fact that the Impersonal God, the Reality, is not limited by any quality of nature, hence not confined by any character of the body, mind, intellect or ego, etc. Even 'He' does not qualify the Supreme, yet we have to use some form of address for our understanding. The Personal God, however, may be conceptualised for visualisation by the human mind with some characterisations, although the qualities – whatever the human mind thinks of God – remain a superimposition as well as an attempt to limit the Limitless!

The subtitle of the book reflects the ultimate aim of our lives. In India and abroad, Hindus and several followers of other faiths know about the *Gita*. The learned ones and those desirous of learning about all the major religions of the world can tell what contains the *Gita*. Yet, because of the complexity of content or the detailed commentaries and intricate religio-philosophical implications, much remains for the layperson to comprehend.

This is particularly so with the younger generation, who have the will to learn but little time or patience to venture deeper. Usually, they realise that the *Gita* advocates 'work but do not desire its fruits' and wonder: how is this possible? Or, 'the Atman is immortal; only it changes the body like worn-out clothes' and wonder: where do I go after my death?

The new generation also has a lot of interest in Yoga, but in its modern, altered form. Alas! It is the new fashion of life to practise Yoga but nothing much is achieved except some relaxation. Yoga is Divine Knowledge without any religious stigma or bias, through which, if understood properly, one can achieve total happiness and fulfilment in life. The *Gita* is a treatise on Yoga.

Keeping this aspect in mind, short, simplified basics of the *Gita* have been compiled in this book. In no way is it a learned commentary, an explanatory series of notes, or an intellectual interpretation – of which I am fully aware. It only puts forth, simply and briefly, the wisdom strewn throughout the *Gita*. It is neither preaching by the author nor an attempt to change your established beliefs; yet it is an attempt to unfold one's personality and bring harmony into life along the lines the great Yogiraj Krishna had narrated four millennia ago. If a person follows even a few directives given by Krishna, he can win the battle against adversities and live a prosperous, happy and peaceful life hereafter. If one goes deeper, he can attain freedom and become one with Pure Consciousness.

That is Salvation!

Contents

Introduction

The antiquity of the *Bhagavad Gita* dates back to about four thousand years or even more. It is a classic divine song based on the dialogue between Krishna and His warrior friend, Arjuna. In its extensive sense, Yoga is the undercurrent theme of the major realms narrated by Krishna, which shall lead to freedom when practised.

Krishna imparts the Divine Knowledge at a very crucial juncture in the centre of the battlefield just before the Mahabharata war between cousins was about to commence over the division of their kingdom. Lord Krishna is an incarnation of the Supreme, in that He is the Yogiraj (the Greatest of Yogis). He was perfectly in tune with the Cosmic Intelligence through His complete establishment in Eternal Yoga; and Arjuna was a mundane prince, shattered on facing the hard reality of life, which challenged him to annihilate his own elders, teachers, friends, and cousins who were ready to fight against him. Although he had an intense desire for victory, the anxiety of the killing and destruction that would follow – even he himself and his four Pandava brothers could be killed – disoriented and confused him. He could not decide whether to fight or to put down his weapons.

At this threshold of emotional distress and mental agony, he put down his bow and arrows, trembling at the thought of the inevitable death, destruction and devastation on both sides of the family and the resulting trauma for those who survived the war. Arjuna felt that even if he were victorious after killing his cousins-turned-enemies and their supporters, he would accumulate great sins and would never be happy although he and his brothers would win back their kingdom from the Kauravas.

Before the declaration of the Mahabharata war, Krishna had exhausted all possible efforts for a peaceful settlement between the two families. As Krishna was related to both the sides and also believed that peace should not be disturbed at any cost, He acted as a mediator. Regrettably, the Kauravas were adamant and inconsiderate. They were not ready to part with any land at all. Therefore, war remained the only way out to settle the issue.

Before the war, Krishna gave both sides the option of choosing either Him or His army to fight on their side. The Kauravas asked for His army to fight on their side. But the Pandavas requested Krishna Himself to be with them, to which He agreed but purely in a non-combatant's role. He took the responsibility of being a charioteer for Arjuna during this war for justice. Krishna was Arjuna's friend, mentor, teacher, guide and philosopher.

Now, as Arjuna stood miserable, indecisive and fearful, Krishna advised him to act and not to worry about the fruits of the action; to witness the episodes of life and death; the cycles of happenings; the ongoing drama of creation, sustenance and dissolution of the universe under the illumination of the Supreme; the ever-changing vicissitude of life in the Cosmic Perspective; and the Immutable, Imperishable Divine Reality. Krishna told him that the only way to overcome his mental agony was to remain poised, unperturbed and calm, abandoning wild desires under all circumstances. And He advised Arjuna to act, and not to react with passion. Such a blissful state of mind could be achieved only through Yoga.

Subsequently, imbibing the teachings of Krishna and 'beholding' the Cosmic Form of the Supreme – which is All-pervading, Beginningless, Limitless, and Endless, in which all are heading towards their terminal fate of death under the sway of Time – Arjuna achieved enlightenment. He experienced that action is the method for breaking the bondage of attachment and knowledge is the only way to dispel the darkness of ignorance. It is an attitude towards life as well as the world that must be changed to purify negative tendencies. Pure Consciousness ever illumines all happenings. This could be realised by concentration of the mind and single-pointedness of purpose.

Ultimately, Arjuna gathered his wits, became calm and composed and thereafter fought with valour to emerge victorious.

In much the same manner, our life is a battlefield. In the ongoing battle between good and evil, we may be involved inadvertently and have to struggle every moment. We have to fight at the physical level to protect our body from hunger, disease and the vagaries of Nature, as well as from anti-social elements and the machines of modern comfort! Our energy dissipates in gathering comforts and luxuries and in protecting them. Mistakenly, we consider our acquirements to be permanent. Alas, in the ever-changing world, nothing is forever. When our material wealth, power and honour, which we earned with great effort, are lost, we become miserable.

At the mental and intellectual levels, our fight goes on with various confused systems of faiths, 'isms', theories, and contradictory ideas about political structures and even science. Such mind-enslaving cults take birth everyday. Yet, we don't get clear answers to our burning questions – Who am I? For what purpose have I come to this world? What is the ultimate aim of my life? Is it simply to eat, drink and remain in sensuality like a beast, or is it something higher? Where does true happiness lie?

These questions haunt us knowingly or unknowingly, and we go on fighting battles in search of that which we do not know! Actually, we all are in search of *ananda*, Bliss, which is our real nature, but very few know this fact and simply grope in the darkness for happiness.

At the emotional level, we are most miserable. Even close relationships fall apart and we are disillusioned; friends or colleagues deceive or misunderstand us; children do not meet our expectations and even our spouse may be unfaithful. What a tragedy!

During our journey of life we ride the raging waves of time, caught up in dualities: happiness-unhappiness, profit-loss, health-sickness, honour-dishonour, heat-cold, love-hate, and innumerable others. The *Gita* teaches one to be balanced and poised even under the influence of contradictory pulls and pressures. But at times, we become desperate like Arjuna! We lose *viveka*, the discriminative intellect, and the objectivity of a situation because our understanding is veiled by selfish attachment.

Thus, we are consumed in the marathon chase after happiness and we may achieve this for a short while. But we forget that nothing is stable in this world and so we are distressed most of the time, if we do not cultivate the power of objectivity about life's realities and the play of the Supreme. We are given tremendous opportunities for spiritual evolution by Nature, but if we don't explore ourselves within, this is our misfortune!

Our wild desires and an ever-wandering mind make us a wreck. The most tragic situation arises when we toil hard at work, hankering for a favourable result under pressure from an agitated mind but we don't get the desired result. In this vicious cycle, we become victims of our own mind, which is conditioned by our ego. The ego, in reality, is our own Self (soul) but it acquires the qualities of gross Nature and is covered by remnant *vaasnas* or tendencies of several planes from past time. Thus, the ego accumulates good or evil happenings. As long as the soul (the Pure Self) within us remains covered by the dark smoke of desires, passion, dullness, lust, greed, and anger, and as long as these traits within us are not purified, the Consciousness within us remains hidden. Therefore, it does not shine forth and shower real happiness and genuine fulfilment, which is His Nature.

In such a situation, Krishna's blissful clairvoyance can come to our rescue. We may remain happy, successful, tranquil and balanced in our life if we practise the essence of the *Gita*. The testimony of this promise is self-evident throughout human history.

Symbolically, our life is like the battlefield of Mahabharata. Our five major senses and their ramifications are the Pandavas (five brothers). In totality, the body, mind, intellect, *chitta*, and the ego are extensions of our experienced world. We are continuously struggling with the hundred demoniac traits (the Kauravas were one hundred brothers) within and without. The chief warrior, Arjuna, is our mind, in conjunction with the intellect and ego. Lord Krishna is Pure Consciousness – the Cosmic Intelligence Who illumines our mind and intellect only when they are purified and cleansed after we surrender unto Him with a prayer to become the charioteer of our life.

In our distress, rejected by the world, we throw away our bow and arrows and perspire with anxiety about the reward or fruits of our action and remain in the dark about our unknown and uncertain destiny. But just as Arjuna surrendered at the altar of the Almighty, if we lay ourselves at His feet, He saves us and ushers enlightenment into our lives. This leads to freedom or salvation.

Today, the *Gita* is no more the monopoly of a single religion or culture; it has crossed all barriers erected by man and acquired a universal character. It is a science of humane thoughts, righteous actions, dynamic living, love and peace, a continuous happiness and Realisation of the Truth. It is also an art of success and happiness for those who adopt the teachings into their life without any bias whatsoever. It is a grand treatise of Cosmic Yoga.

The new age most needs the wisdom of the *Gita* because of eroding value systems, stupendous consumerism, unscrupulous exploitation of Nature resulting in the poisoning of our environment, rocketing passion for sensuality and super-luxury, terror killings in the name of religion, politics or blinkered heroism, and incurable unhappiness in spite of a glut in many aspects of life.

Although better informed and superbly equipped with modern technology, the younger generation is mostly without its bearings in the realm of self-evolution; it is, therefore, to be understood that only knowledge about the Supreme, the Self, the Cosmic Yoga of Krishna, and the value-based living thus achieved, can be helpful in attaining real, stable peace and happiness in all walks of life.

The Yoga as narrated in the *Gita* by Yogiraj Krishna can bring the Eternal Light into the lives of those who practise it in word and deed.

Some Contemporary Thinking

The teachings of the *Gita* prompt one to analyse some facets of the current scenario related to man, society and the environment. Although peripheral thinking, the account given below is nevertheless intimately connected with the thematic development and understanding of the *Gita* with its multiple visions. The following contemporary thoughts also answer several questions that arise in the minds of the younger generation.

The Right to Act But Never to Its Fruits!

One of the key aphorisms in the *Gita* states: "You have the right to act but not to its fruits; therefore, do not hanker for the fruits of action, but also do not get attached to inaction." Through the centuries, the varied interpretations of this *shloka* have at times generated contradictory thinking.

How could one work without a desire for rewards? Is it possible to exert sincerely and diligently without any motivation? However, the essence of this wisdom lies in the concept of non-attachment. From amongst all the creatures of the creation known so far, only humans possess the freedom to act deliberately and innovatively. Therefore, they should make proper use of this right given by the Almighty for the purpose of realising the Self. Even if he so wishes, man cannot forgo action and if at all he abandons action, he has to face adverse consequences and miseries. Therefore, one must act continuously and work in the right direction, urged the scriptures as well as enlightened ones.

Howsoever dexterously he acts to achieve them, desirable achievements may elude man. If one always dreams or has strong longings for the fruits of his action, the resultant agitation, anxiety, worries and disturbance further mars one's success. Fear of failure dissipates concentration and focus that is an essential ingredient for success. Hence, the *Gita* advises one not to worry about the outcome of your action, which is beyond your control and thereby makes you miserable if you fail, but to act and act forcefully, intelligently, and untiringly, without losing one's peace of mind.

Such an approach improves the chances of success, and even if you are unsuccessful despite your best efforts, still do not take it to heart as a disaster because you do not have the right to demand the fruits of your action. This is the law of veiled destiny. Furthermore, even if disgusted with failures, you should still not stop working, because abandoning action is *tamas* – the realm of ignorance and darkness that results in immense unhappiness.

We must dedicate every action to the Supreme. We always think that we are the 'doers', the 'achievers', and the 'possessors'. But on deeper contemplation it is revealed that none of these three conditions exists in reality. They are a mirage of your mind – always changing, shifting, appearing and disappearing. It is the combination of innumerable strings in the array of happenings that apparently makes you a 'doer', 'achiever' and 'possessor' – that too, prone to continued vacillation. Nature controls this system.

Therefore, surrender the action as well as its result unto Nature – an expression of the Almighty. Liberate yourself from anxiety, worry, disturbing thoughts and agitation about the morrow, and fly free after performing conscientiously. This shall cleanse your mind of clutter and make it serene and balanced. The equipoise of the mind, even under crushing pressure of dualities, is Yoga.

You must undertake your duties and face your responsibilities – boldly, squarely and intelligently. You must never be dull, lethargic or fatalistic. This creates a daydream that is another form of bondage. Don't abandon your righteous performance, propriety and faith; else you will land in the wilderness of fear and the emptiness of frustration.

You may feel discouraged if not motivated by the desire for the fruits of your endeavour. Seeking the fruits of your endeavour may seem correct. But it is not so. You have to readjust your bearings in this regard. The emphasis of negation should be on the anxiety about the outcome, not on the goal, the action, the motivation and the ultimate achievement. Aim at your goal with steady concentration, focus only on the bull's-eye – and shoot! Don't tremble in advance thinking about failing or winning. This is the Yoga of Action.

The central idea of this aphorism is towards performing one's duty selflessly, wisely and skilfully. The ego of the doership must be laid at His feet; subsequently, attachment to expected fruits would automatically be dissolved. Thus did Krishna enlighten Arjuna, who ultimately acquired this Karma Yoga, the actionless action.

Unfortunately, a fatalistic approach leading to inaction had doomed the Indian psyche into a dark period for several centuries. The dynamic teachings of *Vedanta* and the *Gita* were either misunderstood or misinterpreted for selfish goals of its custodians. *Bhagya* (fate) became the key word in the lives of the masses, consequently bringing miseries, defeats, insults and embarrassments. Laziness overshadowed the desire for a better quality of life. Karma Yoga (the Yoga of selfless action) became Karam Yoga (the Yoga of *bhagya* or fate). The ignorant were exploited under the guise of *bhagya*.

In view of this pathetic illusion, we must rise to the occasion and act... skilfully. *Yogah Karmasu Kaushlam* (*Gita* 2/50): the work done with dexterity, artistically, in harmony with the environs and by and large for the benefit of all

Creation is the real Yoga. This can be achieved by balanced thinking, a forceful and planned attitude, and deep concentration on the goal, an efficient mindset and unwavering commitment without the fear of failure. This is Krishna Yoga comprising all the Yogas known so far. Such a state of mind comes only when there is no *raga* (attachment, self-gratification) with favourable results, and *dwesha* (hatred, jealousy) for the unwanted outcome.

When one surrenders the fruits of his expertise at the feet of the Almighty, only then is such a state of the Self revealed. Such an action guarantees four *purusharthas* (vital attainments): *artha* (prosperity), *dharma* (harmony with Nature by law of purity), *kama* (fulfilment), and *moksha* (salvation).

Mansa–Vaacha–Karmana: Gateway to Salvation

Twentieth century researches in sub-atomic particle physics have proved that the ultimate constituent of "matter" behaves in an uncertain pattern, i.e., during the experiment if the investigator thinks that particle could act as 'matter', it behaves like 'matter' and if he wishes it to act like 'energy', the particle gives the results of energy. The direction of rotation of these sub-atomic bodies is also generally guided by the thought of the experimenter. Baffled by this behaviour of matter, scientists theorised that the consciousness of the researcher might be guiding the pathways of matter through enormous speed. At this point, particle physics enters the realm of the mind, which is a reflection of the Infinite Energy.

Our central point here is the process of "thinking" which is monitored by the mind (*mansa*). The mind generates immense energy in the process of thought-making. It is the source of all happenings (good or evil, pleasant or unpleasant) and these events behave in the same way as sub-atomic particles do – their mode of existence is determined by the mind. Likewise, the episodes of life are neither pleasant nor unpleasant in the timeless vicissitude of the universe but they are what your mind thinks them to be, just as the particle of an electron of the atom behaves on the lines of thought of the experimenter.

Further, according to the quantum theory, it has been formulated that energy never vanishes – it gets transmuted into another form of energy, or fuses to become mass (matter) and vice versa; mass gets altered into energy by fusion as has been recently postulated in the case of continued energy of the sun.

The energy of *mansa* is derived from the Eternal Energy Fountain; it gets transformed into the energy of *vaacha* (speech), which in turn manifests into *karmana* (action) and then the act goes on generating mental or physical formations. Through contemplation of the Supreme, enlightened sages have realised that the stream of thought-speech-act constitutes a bundle of energies (*oorja* or *shakti*), which further creates tendencies (*vaasnas*), a variant of energy, and ultimately your *karmas* are cast. *Karma* is nothing but a quantum of *vaasnas* thus accumulated (*sanchit*) through time, at the ultra-micro-plane of being, and manifests at the right time of its sprouting, giving you results, the good or evil quality of which is experienced according to the bent of your mind. If there is no mind, *karma* is annihilated!

However, realised sages did not stop here. They ushered worldly people – like most of us – into the path of salvation (*nirvana*). They have flowed the spring of Absolute Knowledge, the nectar of *gyana*, to quench the thirst of mundane people who normally don't aspire to attain salvation. This wisdom reveals that *nirvana* can be attained through discriminative knowledge; darkness can be driven away from your house even by a tiny earthen lamp of bright light and not by a broom or stick or by howling! Such light of knowledge is contained within the pure mind. Therefore, prudence lies in self-purification and contemplation so that the energy of thought is channelled into a proper path before it goes astray. This wisdom has been elaborated in the *Gita*.

How can one do it? This appears mystical – a task that could probably be undertaken only by yogis or renunciates! But this is not really so. The learned have shown us the way through their brilliant insight. To purify your mind-speech-act through meditation, Krishna advocates concentration; Buddha says to watch your breathing mentally. Christ wants you to empty yourself and only then will you be filled with Grace. Ramana Maharshi advises you to question yourself: "Who am I?" Vivekananda recommends watching the train of your thoughts from a distance. And Jiddu Krishnamurti wants you to make your mind unconditioned of the past. Such practice shall cleanse the thoughts and sieve the speech to make it loving, compassionate, balanced and soothing. An intensive, rigorous vigilance on the mind and speech will thus lead to humane, egoless action; you can neither harm others nor create unpleasant situations. Even if this happens, you remain calm and tranquil because of your direct attunement with the Eternal Intelligence of the Infinite Energy. Krishna advocates alternative methods of Yoga – whichever suits your temperament – to attain success in keeping your equipoise in all contradictory situations in life.

Love and compassion become your natural tendencies. Thus, no *vaasna*-energy is further accumulated, hence no *karmas* are generated. So also, the energy of old *karma* gets exhausted and transformed into all-bliss happiness. And fully controlled by your thoughts, a live quietude prevails in your life. What else could be the gateway to salvation? *Gita* ushers you into this gateway!

Survival of the Fittest: A Paradox

During the latter-half of the nineteenth century, the theory of the Origin of Species was propounded, based on the principle of an ongoing *struggle for existence* amongst organisms in Nature, ensuring *survival of the fittest*. These two aphorisms remained benchmarks of the theory of evolution, although several new concepts were added to the module of evolution during the twentieth century. 'Survival of the fittest', in its simplest form, means that only the most fit organisms – plants or animals, including man – shall survive; the weaklings will die off.

Our focal point for the present is man – *Homo sapiens* – to which all of us belong. The most intelligent creature, man, is no doubt also the fittest. At the present juncture, there is little challenge to man from other species or Nature for survival, as he has conquered almost the entire globe.

But all through the centuries of human history man has been engaging in warfare with his own kind. Obviously, this is because of the lack of divine knowledge. Hatred and greed-based fights for territories and empires, wealth and women and for dominating fellow-members of the species is now threatening the planet. In this process, man has en masse disturbed the delicate balance of ecological systems and polluted seas, rivers, soil, air and space and, above all, his own conscience.

Despite the presence of great thinkers, *avatars,* messiahs and prophets, born from time to time to advocate peace and love, men have fought bitterly amongst themselves to achieve supremacy of biased faith in their own religion, in political systems or in some other way. In spite of knowing that the fundamental principles of all religions and faiths are similar in that they aim for the welfare of the human race, men have been blowing up trivial differences out of all proportion.

Although the future is always uncertain and no prophecy can ever be absolutely correct, but given the present set of systems and the general trend of behaviour of *Homo sapiens,* it seems plausible that mass extinction of humankind will occur at some point of time. The doomsday could be one million years away from now or even less.

But can Nature go so wrong by programming *hara-kiri* for her most intelligent species? If not, what is the hidden agenda for mankind? To my mind, it still remains the survival of the fittest! Then who is the fittest? Is it one of the various political despots and dictators, varied political 'isms' or any of the religious 'isms'? None of them, because all have collapsed or are collapsing one by one under their own weight. People who are intelligent, honest, compassionate and loving with tremendous awareness about the harmony with the Reality of the Universe and the Self – the light of all beings – shall survive, as they are the fittest and support the noble cause of Nature. All selfish and unscrupulous members of humankind shall perish by the sting of their own *karma*. This is not wishful thinking but an observation based on the laws of adaptability, flexibility, compatibility, and harmony, which monitor social evolution.

Krishna narrates in the *Gita* that His devotee does not perish. One who has a pure heart and is established in Yoga and has *sattvic* traits, only he can be His devotee. Nature is the creation of the Supreme and her programme cannot be erroneous.

Of course, the curse of group misdeeds and collective sinning has to be borne by the innocent also but the ultimate survivors will be those who support the continuance of Nature's righteous traits for the next level of evolution to come.

Chapter 1

The Horror of Life's Problems

In the kingdom of Hastinapur (a place near New Delhi), Pandu and Dhritarashtra were two prince brothers; the former had five sons called the Pandavas, and the latter had one hundred, known as the Kauravas. Pandu died young and Dhritarashtra, though blind since birth, was enthroned as the king. Although they had grown up together, the Kauravas always nurtured jealousy, ill will and vindictiveness against the Pandavas and never wanted to share the kingdom with them. However, the Pandavas were more powerful, upright and righteous. Such was the seed of dispute that grew into a thorny issue leading to the Mahabharata (The Great War of India) between cousins. The Kauravas were selfish, unscrupulous and wicked to the extent that they betrayed the Pandavas, tried to disrobe the Pandavas' wife, Draupadi, and by deceit secured a promise of twelve years' exile from the latter.

Krishna, the personified Eternal Yogiraj attuned with Pure Consciousness, was very intimate with the Pandavas and a bosom friend of Arjuna – the third brother amongst the Pandavas – and the sustainer of social propriety, justice, righteousness and peace. After the return of the Pandavas from exile, when peace talks could yield no results to solve the discord between the cousins, the Mahabharata war was declared. Both armies comprised common elders, teachers, relations and friends. The Kauravas had several warriors whom Arjuna revered, but since they were in the service of the king, they had to remain allied with the Kauravas. Krishna was on the side of the Pandavas as a non-combatant – only driving Arjuna's chariot during the war that lasted 18 days.

On the first day of the war, both the forces stood arrayed against each other, blowing conches and horns that made thunderous sounds, a customary practice in those days, declaring their readiness to fight on the battlefield of Kurukshetra. Arjuna requested Krishna to drive his chariot into the open space between the two formations of archers and soldiers. At this juncture, Arjuna had a full view of the army of the Kauravas at close quarters; and seeing his near-and-dear ones in the opposite camp, with whom he was supposed to wage war, he broke down emotionally.

Arjuna lamented to Krishna that he did not want to kill his kinsmen in order to have the pleasure of regaining their kingdom. The destruction of his kith and kin would be a heinous sin. It was against *dharma* i.e., the righteous and essential moral fabric of society, or Law of Being; and such extermination of mighty members of society would result in a chaotic situation and immorality.

Arjuna was so overpowered by compassion and depression that he put his weapons down and sat with trembling limbs. Krishna then spoke up and now shines the wisdom of the *Gita* to show the path by dispelling the darkness of ignorance, fear and attachment.

This is the essence of the first chapter of the *Gita*, entitled *Depression of Arjuna*.

We are play things in the hands of circumstances in life that are continuously changing. Some call it destiny or fate, while others explain it as a dynamic arrangement of physical, mental or emotional attributes within and without us. However, whatsoever philosophy we believe in, we have to face the challenges of oddities and threatening circumstances all through our lifetime. In spite of our following the path of ethical codes, problems will arise and denounce us at times. Be that as it may, we have to fight them out. Most often, one has to take hard and unpleasant decisions against one's own people and beloved persons that may not conform to one's inner voice. Caught in the cyclone of the onslaught of forces of anti-happiness on several occasions, one gets dejected with the world and drops out of the mainstream of life!

Such situations, behaving as enemies, are hundreds; they are mighty and appear to be invincible. The opponents could be persons whom you loved and believed trustworthy, but you are betrayed, cheated and deceived by them for no fault of yours. You become disillusioned. (This was the mental state of Arjuna.) The Mahabharata of life is constantly going on. The good and evil forces are perpetually clashing.

A breakdown in finances, health, love, honour, prestige and values may make you an Arjuna. You throw your weapons down and collapse under the crushing pressure of indecision. And here comes the *Gita* to rescue you, to make you stand up on your feet and to get you ready to fight your way out of the crisis. The *Gita Gyana* (Blissful Knowledge showered by Cosmic Intelligence), when imbibed in your personality, will transform your being into an ecstatic state of Realisation.

Gita Gyana 1

- ❑ **1.1:** Be intensely aware – moment-to-moment – about the forthcoming odd situations in life.
- ❑ **1.2:** Do not believe dishonest and unfaithful persons even if they are close to you.
- ❑ **1.3:** Take the disputed issue up to the threshold of a peaceful settlement.
- ❑ **1.4:** If you are pitched against an unscrupulous situation or person and cannot get out of the mud, fight with all your valour and might – not half-heartedly.

- ❑ **1.5:** In the cosmic arrangements of happenings, you must act and not throw away your weapons.
- ❑ **1.6:** Your discriminative intelligence is your charioteer that functions efficiently when you are calm and poised, unagitated and serene.
- ❑ **1.7:** Act – do not react.
- ❑ **1.8:** A battle for justice and righteous causes leads to peace and harmony.
- ❑ **1.9:** Do not collapse under the pressure of indecision; decide and perform.
- ❑ **2.0:** Stand erect and face the situation, keeping faith in the Supreme.

> **1. Let your drive for vigorous performance be driven by Cosmic Intelligence.**

Chapter 2

Knowledge is Pivotal

Knowledge is the key to happiness. The warrior prince Arjuna was unhappy because his attunement with the Divine Knowledge of Being was veiled with attachment and emotions. He was extremely sorrowful because of the awkward situation in which he found himself on the battlefield. He continues to lament under the pressure of emotions and melancholy.

Krishna asks Arjuna wherefrom the weakness of the heart has overwhelmed him – the bravest of the braves. Such a condition is disgraceful for Arjuna who was a great warrior and invincible. But Arjuna continues to argue that how can he fight and kill those he worships, adores and loves. Filled with indecision, he requests Krishna to guide him about the right action at this crucial moment.

Krishna affectionately introduces Arjuna to the paths of Knowledge, Action, Devotion and Renunciation. He narrates that the Reality is indestructible; the Divine Energy is eternal, so why should one grieve for the living or the dead? The world of objects, including our body, is impermanent and ever changing, while the Self is Immortal, Eternal and Immutable. Nobody kills, neither is anybody killed in the total cosmic perspective; the *atman* (Inner Self, Soul) of the worldly being casts off the body as we do worn-out clothes and wear new ones; this process goes on *ad infinitum*. Weapons cannot pierce the *atman*, fire is incapable of burning it, and water cannot make it wet. The Self is timeless and without origin or extinction, hence one should not grieve if one has knowledge of this Truth.

Being a warrior, Arjuna is advised to follow his sacred duty and fight this war to establish justice and righteous order in society. Else, he shall face dishonour and disgrace that is worse than death. Keeping equipoise in pain and pleasure, loss and profit, defeat and victory, actions to kill his kin-turned-enemies will not generate sin, i.e., self-condemning guilt.

Krishna further enlightens Arjuna about the Yoga of Action. The path of Yoga, in brief, comprises a single-pointed, concentrated dedication of body, mind, intellect and ego in attaining union of the Self with the Supreme. In other words, to establish oneness of your being with Truth or the Eternal. The Yoga of Action aims at consistency in duty without the worry of its fruits. At the same time, there must be no attachment with inaction. The performance of action without attachment to the outcome and a commitment to remain unperturbed in case of success or failure are the basics of Karma Yoga (the Yoga of Action). Such an evenness of mind mastered by penetrating intelligence gathers no sin of bad deeds. Furthermore, dexterity in one's action and expertise in performance are also attributes of Karma Yoga.

On listening to the unfolding of steady wisdom and the process of merging with the Superconscious State, Arjuna wants to know of such a yogi (one who is established in Yoga) who becomes steadfast in such a state of mind and action. Krishna elaborates: A yogi of steady wisdom is one who abandons desire, fear, anger, hankering after mundane pleasures and who is also above joy or hate while performing actions in the world. Uncontrolled desires and wild senses sway the minds of even wise men; this creates delusion and loss of discrimination. Such a turbulent state of the mind leads to annihilation of one's personality. Therefore, for attaining perpetual peace and tranquillity, one must be detached from desires and only after this stage shall one be led to happiness.

The self-controlled person is alive and aware of the recurrently altering attributes of the world and the causes of agitation in the mind while others are blindfolded in their ego sense, thus being exhausted miserably in chasing the mirage of happiness in worldly affairs – where there is no peace. The one who is steadfast in such wisdom attains union with *Brahman* – the Superconsciousness of the cosmos.

This is the essence of the second chapter of the *Gita*, entitled *The Yoga of Knowledge*.

Only a source of light can remove pitch darkness in a room – not thorough cleaning by a broom. Divine Knowledge is this kindled light of Self-realisation. It is not merely garbage of junk information. In the perplexity of life's battlefield, when the mind falls in disarray losing its bearings and the ability to diagnose the 'illness', Divine Knowledge of the *Gita* ushers in the enlightened path of peace and happiness.

A constant change in the world is occurring against the changeless backdrop of the Supreme. The totality of cosmic energy remains constant, so why lament the living or the departed? Take it as a drama of Eternal Power. One must not grieve to the extent of disintegration. All the dualities of world experience – profit and loss, life and death, honour and dishonour – have a beginning and an end; they are impermanent; therefore, one must not anchor with them. The Self is Immortal and Real, Indestructible and Imperishable, Changeless and Eternal; the body, mind, intellect and the ego are continuously changing; perpetual alteration is their nature, hence they are not real and, therefore, destined for doom.

One has a right to work, to act and to act with all his vigour, but he does not possess the right to the outcome of his action. Thus, expectations should be surrendered to the will of the Supreme. One must not be unhappy or sorrowful, even if the results are unfavourable. That is not your right, besides not being in your hands. However, one must work with all the expertise at one's command because working with excellence is in itself an essential component of Yoga. Put all the resources and concentration into the job at hand but remain unattached to the outcome; such an attitude shall not generate anxiety for the future and shall not push you into uncertainty and restlessness. This is the Yoga of Action in competence and skill. It keeps you in the present – not in the past or in the future.

The expert management of money, residence, security, relationships, progress and planning in the world around is essential but the management of emotions, feelings, love, depression, dejection, fear, dishonour, disbalance and distress within you is still important for stable happiness. The *Gita* advises one to go beyond all evils, delusion, unrighteous pleasures and unintelligent gratifications of sensory organs. Enjoy life with restraint on the senses, free from extreme repulsion and attraction. This shall bring peace and tranquillity of mind, happiness and wisdom and make for successful living. The ultimate goal of life is to attain peace, but the materialistic means to achieve this goal should not consume your personality and toss you into the turbulence of ups-and-downs, leaving the shore of peace and happiness away. Although money may be necessary for some happiness, it is not necessary that stable happiness will come only through money.

Rising above the opposite forces of dual nature, one must be intensively aware of the drama going around him; one must play the role of an actor – now weeping, now laughing, but always attuned with the direction of the Self, not losing the identity of the Self within which is the witness of all happenings. Control your mind through Yoga and control the world; be in harmony with Nature and achieve non-fleeting happiness.

Gita Gyana 2

- ❑ **2.1:** Divine Knowledge is the key to stable happiness.
- ❑ **2.2:** Discriminative intelligence can usher in the knowledge of Reality.
- ❑ **2.3:** In the total cosmic perspective, the Truth is Indestructible, Energy is Imperishable and the Self is Timeless.
- ❑ **2.4:** Act with dexterity, skill being also a component of Yoga, without generating anxiety about the fruits of the action. Manage your inner world efficiently as you do your outer world.
- ❑ **2.5:** Abandon uncontrolled, turbulent desires; they lead to agony of the mind. Make them a disciplined force, and win.
- ❑ **2.6:** Attain perennial peace by unplugging your thought-current from mundane pleasures and pains.
- ❑ **2.7:** Be in immense awareness towards perpetual changes in the physical and mental world.
- ❑ **2.8:** Don't chase the mirage of pseudo-happiness that is doomed to vanish; create peace within by Yoga.
- ❑ **2.9:** Don't believe blindly in fate but depend on intuition and clairvoyance – achieved through Yoga – about the universal scheme of things.
- ❑ **3.0:** Control your mind to control the world.

> **2. Don't let your happy present be torn apart by backward pulls of repentance or regret for the 'past' and forward pushes of anxiety for the 'future'.**

Chapter 3

Action is the Method

We have seen that Krishna introduced Arjuna to the Yoga of Knowledge, with a lace of the Yoga of Action. However, Arjuna could not comprehend that the action is not opposed but complementary to knowledge. Perplexed, he asks Krishna which of these paths is superior and which one he should follow at this juncture.

At this, Krishna replies that both non-performance of action as well as renunciation (*sannyas*) of the world lead to futility. Moreover, one cannot remain without performing action even for a moment, because one is continuously propelled by Nature to do so. Therefore, action is superior to non-action if performed with a sense of detachment and a disciplined mind devoted to Karma Yoga. Such *karma* generates no bondage leading to unhappiness if the work is done with a feeling of service and dedication to the welfare of the family, society, living beings and the environment at large. All these attributes are contained in *yagna*, i.e., mutually beneficial, social undertaking. The outcome of any good work should be shared for the well-being of the family as well as the needy in society.

An unselfish attitude in the ordained distribution of opportunities, thus generated, shall result in the happiness of humanity. From the Supreme Creator to the tiniest creature, all are bound to the wheel of action and are mutual benefactors; this sustains the system of existence of the cosmos. One who does not follow this circle of reciprocal support, but instead remains engaged in his sensual, selfish gratification and self-enjoyment commits sin (i.e., self-hurting guilt and agitation, turbulence of mind). Ultimately, such a person cannot secure peace and happiness. On the contrary, one who performs action without attachment attains the Supreme.

Krishna further enlightens Arjuna on the mandatory aspect of action by saying that He (Krishna, ever abiding in the Supreme Consciousness) has nothing to perform obligatorily but even then He works; else the world takes a negative signal of non-performance. Krishna exhorts Arjuna to act and fight by resigning the outcome of actions unto Him and with a concentrated mind on the Self, to be free from fear and without the ego sense of the doer. Love and hate, or attachment and aversion are experiences of the human senses; therefore, they should not come in the way of duty because they create obstacles in the path of Realisation, even for well-informed and learned minds. One must follow one's own way of life and the Law of Righteous Living (*dharma*) and perform his duty rather than wish to follow another's way of life, howsoever tempting it may appear.

On being asked about the nature of the instinct which forces a person to commit evil deeds, even against his own will, Krishna answers that lust, anger and low, basic impulses prompt one to act unwisely under the force of desire and to accrue sin, because his rationality gets veiled by negative tendencies at the time of committing bad deeds. Such desires originate from the senses, the mind and intellect leading to a disability in one's faculty of judgement. In the hierarchy of the body, senses, mind and intellect, the last one is on top but the *atman* is superior to the intellect. Krishna tells Arjuna that by knowing the *atman* (the soul within), which illumines all other faculties, he should control and discipline desires, although it is difficult to conquer them.

This is the essence of the third chapter of the *Gita*, entitled *The Yoga of Action*.

Selfless activity makes the mind peaceful and, likewise, meditation upon Pure Consciousness brings blissful happiness. Thus, both action and knowledge are essential to experience the Absolute. Performance is needed for worldly systems, and it is a way to Realisation as well. Running away from problems and challenges of the world is no renunciation. Every particle in the universe is in a state of motion and action. This is the Law of Nature.

So, one must act, and act intelligently, detached and fearless, devoted to Karma Yoga. Such a person excels in his undertakings and remains established in the Supreme. Working with the spirit of *yagna* is superior to all activities; in modern terms, *yagna* is a benevolent effort for the welfare of the family, society and humanity, the world of the living and non-living, and the environment. The gains of *yagna* must be shared mutually, particularly with the needy. Thus, harmony and peace could be established amongst people of various nations and the environment of the world could be saved. This is the ultimate goal of Action and Knowledge. Proper distribution of blessings obtained from *yagna* means dissemination of opportunities for work, education, health, security, shelter, etc, which are the real attributes of *yagna*.

Nature and the environment must be preserved with care and tenderness by contributing a share from our achievements. To disturb the lithosphere, biosphere and atmosphere is anti-*yagna* activity – an unrighteous act and unintelligent derangement of the life so meticulously ordained by the Supreme. The selfish act of exploitation of animals, forests, water resources, mountains, etc, brings discordance and catastrophe.

Set lofty ideals in life so that others may follow the same. The learned and the wise should not confuse simple and inexperienced people who are apparently 'attached' to their work for 'selfish' reasons, because all actions are prompted by the qualities of thoughts and ego of the performer. Instead, they should be ushered smoothly into the knowledge of non-attachment by the realised ones.

The mind should be focused on the centre-of-the-being and one must practise to be free from self-aggrandisement. The remnant of the ego is helpful in the journey through Time if channelled in the right direction. Such a state could be obtained only by constant practice. It must be understood that passion and aversion for any person, object or situation originate from the fantasy of the five senses; hence, the senses should be disciplined. When uncontrolled, unjust and wild desires remain unfulfilled, anger arises, which is the greatest enemy of self-development. The power of analysing a situation becomes dim because of the smoke of anger. If one is always aware about his *atman* (the Supreme within you) that illumines one's mind and the thinking faculty, and if one is in constant touch with the core of his being, observing the play of phenomena of the world around him, he comes out a winner.

Gita Gyana 3

- ❑ **3.1:** Knowledge is the best tool to establish peace.
- ❑ **3.2:** Unattached action is complementary to knowledge to achieve happiness.
- ❑ **3.3:** Running away from challenges is no renunciation (*tyaga*).
- ❑ **3.4:** A follower of Karma Yoga excels in all undertakings in the world.
- ❑ **3.5:** *Yagna* – a philanthropic performance for mutual benefit in society – brings harmony.
- ❑ **3.6:** Sharing of blessings (outcome) of an action as a *yagna* amongst animates, the inanimate and the environment brings prosperity.
- ❑ **3.7:** Proper and judicious distribution of opportunities is the real attribute of *yagna*.
- ❑ **3.8:** Based on your virtues and selfless work, set high ideals for the less knowledgeable.
- ❑ **3.9:** The senses must be disciplined, desires and anger checked, and a constant touch with the centre-of-your-being maintained.

- ❑ **4.0:** Contemplate on the *atman*; it is the Greatest; be with Him and you become the Greatest.

3. The quality of *karma* (actions) generates the quality of *karma* (destiny).

Chapter 4

Self-perfection is the Technique

So far, Karma Yoga has been introduced to Arjuna followed by a reference to the path of contemplation and meditation. Now, Krishna delves into the origin of this knowledge of Truth, which leads to self-perfection. He states that the Imperishable Yoga, the Primordial Knowledge, originated concurrently with Creation. The Supreme passed it on to the Sun (i.e., the Supreme Brilliance of Energy) and subsequently it was inherited through innumerable generations till now.

Krishna elaborates further that whenever there is a decline and disarray in the righteous way of life and the virtuous system of living, Supreme Consciousness (in which Krishna was firmly established) manifests in the form of Godheads, sages or saints in order to re-establish the right way of living and to provide protection to the ethical order. He who is aware of this action of the Supreme attains Realisation. The one who is detached from attractions and aversions, free from fear and anger, and has surrendered to His will attains Him. Krishna declares that variable patterns of human thinking germinate from their varied mental set-ups, inherent tendencies and accumulated *karma*, destiny, steered by the imprints of good or evil deeds on their psyche through several planes of existence in the past.

Krishna clarifies that one who cultivates intensive awareness about the Presiding Light within oneself and retains equipoise during vigorous action, recognises inaction in the action; in other words, he acts but remains non-entangled; likewise, action in inaction could be identified in the quietude, utter silence of mind and meditative state of contemplation on to the Reality. Such states of action or inaction do not generate *karma* – good or evil.

A Karma Yogi (one who practises the Yoga of Action) is ever content, consequently he craves nothing; his desires are disciplined, hence he gathers no sin though apparently he acts in the world. The one who is complacent over his achievements, not tortured by the dualities of experiences, e.g., profit and loss, birth and death, honour and dishonour, etc, balanced in success and failure and who abides by knowledge of the Self, is a free and liberated being. *Brahman* (Absolute) is to be seen in all actions. Freedom and joy could be achieved in the inner life of a man by burning his sensual cravings in the fire of self-control and the heat of knowledge.

Self-perfection can be accomplished by several techniques, involving physical, mental and intellectual practices. Yoga is one of the prime techniques for such an achievement. It makes one's mind tranquil and pure, thus suitable for higher launching towards Realisation.

There are several types of sacrifices or offerings but sacrifice of ignorance into the knowledge is the greatest. One must see all things in the Self and then in the Supreme. Such knowledge shall make a man free from all fears and tortures of the mind, and bring eternal peace. Against the backdrop of knowledge of the Supreme, actions do not generate *karma* and hence one is liberated. Knowledge of the real nature of the Self, i.e., Self-realisation, is the highest achievement and the greatest possession of one's life. Such Divine Knowledge resides in the Self and can be unveiled through perfection in Yoga. The man who is full of faith and devotion and who has restrained his sensory cravings accrues such knowledge that, in turn, leads to perennial peace. But the ignorant having no faith achieves no peace, neither in this nor in the other world.

He who has relinquished the fruits of his actions through Yoga, removed all doubts through knowledge and become vigilant and awake in the Self is a liberated sage, although he may act in the world. Therefore, retreat into Yoga, establish the self in Divine Knowledge and act vigorously, but unattached, in this world.

This is the essence of the fourth chapter of the *Gita*, entitled *The Yoga of Divine Knowledge.*

The knowledge of Yoga is ancient. The Sun is the symbolic phenomenon of the Supreme Knowledge available to us for direct experience of the power of the Almighty. Thus, Divine Knowledge should be obtained from an experienced person, brilliant like the Sun. Before practising Yoga, one must cleanse one's mind, the inner world, and connect it with the Self.

Supreme Consciousness manifests itself in all periods of time through its play in this world to reaffirm the righteous way of living. He does so whenever there is large-scale decay of virtues and justice in society. Thus, the noble and virtuous are protected and the Law of Being and Ethics is saved from annihilation.

We may experience all sorts of positive and negative emotions while managing our lives in this world, yet if we are profoundly aware about them through our knowledge and if we surrender all our actions unto Him, we are not bound by such sentiments; such a mind becomes suitable for Realisation of the Truth. The performance of action is a prerequisite for our sustenance. Everybody does so, goaded by his natural mindset (*gunas*) but he who abandons the yearning for the fruits of action always remains happy.

Be contemplative about the inner life, the universe and the phenomenon of existence, and live with a sense of detachment striking a balance between worldly affairs and Consciousness by way of the power of discrimination.

For attaining peace and happiness, one must support the needy and the destitute by advice, charity and kindness;

also, through self-denial and austerity in reasonable degrees, evolving ourselves through the devotion and the practice of Yoga, sustained reading and reflection on the writings of great men, and the continuous weeding of ignorance and misconceptions by analytic methods, which are essential to obtain calmness of mind and the subsequent journey for self-development, inner growth and Realisation of *Brahman* – the Truth.

Actions arise from desires and wild desires give rise to ignoble actions; therefore, right knowledge shall regulate desires so that wrong-doings are not manifested. This is so because even fabulous wealth cannot bring peace of mind and happiness if not associated with knowledge of the Self.

Understand that all beings are interwoven by one single, Supreme Consciousness. Thus, realise the Eternal Wisdom and attain calmness that is essential for worldly success, happiness as well as spiritual contentment. Our Inner Self is the abode of knowledge. It can be unveiled by constant and unabated practice of Yoga. By such conceptual perception, the ego is cleansed through the inner Divine experience, which shines forth brightly by the light of *atman*. Then, success is yours.

Gita Gyana 4

- ❑ **4.1:** Yoga is very ancient wisdom.
- ❑ **4.2:** Whenever there is chaos in the righteous way of living, Supreme Consciousness manifests Itself to ordain the systems.
- ❑ **4.3:** To achieve success, one must be free from fear, anger, senseless attractions, bitter aversions, and wild longings.
- ❑ **4.4:** Cultivate intensive awareness about the life-sustaining spark within yourself.
- ❑ **4.5:** Be content with your achievements, without abandoning action for progress and prosperity in the outer as well as the inner world.

- ❑ **4.6:** Do not be torn by pairs of opposite experiences coming in your way.
- ❑ **4.7:** Self-control, channelled by balanced thinking, makes you free and fearless.
- ❑ **4.8:** Make your mind tranquil and pure by practising contemplation and by silencing thought waves, at times.
- ❑ **4.9:** Support the destitute with kindness; observe austerity; reflect on the Eternal Wisdom, and merge with the Consciousness through Yoga for self-development and peace.
- ❑ **5.0:** All particles in the cosmos are interwoven by a single, indestructible energy field, the All-pervading Consciousness; affirm this knowledge for material success, mental happiness, stable peace and spiritual contentment.

4. There is no knowing Him unless you become knowledgeable about your Self.

Chapter 5

Renounce and be Liberated!

As Arjuna's mind was highly disturbed when his chariot was driven into the midst of the two armies, Krishna's preaching so far could not make him decide whether renunciation (*sannyas*) is superior or action. Therefore, he requests Krishna again for clear advice about which of the two ways he must follow.

On hearing his doubt, Krishna says that the Yoga of Action is superior to Renunciation of Action. Here, Krishna means that, for a beginner, action (without attachment) is essential for exhausting his cravings and desires; such a performance shall subdue his I-ness and make him ready for renunciation of the internal agitated state and high-pitched emotions. Renunciation does not mean that one should abandon his action; it means abandoning of inner *dwandas* (pairs of contradictory experiences). A person is considered firmly established in *sannyas* (renunciation) if he feels neither intensive like nor hateful dislike, and is not ruffled by dual factors of opposite nature. In this way, while practising the Yoga of Action, one subtly enters into the Yoga of Renunciation. The mind becomes purified and clean while performing action, thus it is fit for contemplation. Therefore, the ultimate aim is to get rid of internal contradictions and conflicts through exhaustion of desires and *vaasnas* (subtle tendencies) by vigorous actions, with a quiet mind and serene purity of thoughts; such a state escorts you towards Realisation of the Omnipresent, Pure Consciousness.

Krishna further states that an enlightened person will not behave like a high-headed egotist although he performs several acts – voluntary or involuntary – through senses of the body, or by mind and intellect. Peace belongs to him who lives in harmony with himself as well as the world, without being lost in it.

Further, Krishna tells Arjuna about a deeper implication of his teaching that the Supreme does not do anything – neither actions nor involvement in their fruits; it is Nature which acts and our ego which feels – good or evil – about them. Pure Consciousness within all beings remains an Observer. The Eternal Principle does not get involved in the finite happenings of the world because He is Infinite. How can He share your good or bad deeds, or the results thereof? Only our knowledge about the Eternal Power is veiled by ignorance; hence, we suffer. He whose intellect, ego and existence is merged with That realises That and achieves permanent tranquillity in the Self. The knowledgeable and the wise person recognises the presence of a single Divinity in *Brahman*, in all animates and low- or high-ranking human beings. All are equal in the eyes of a wise man, illumined by the Supreme Light.

A man of equipoise and unshakable intellect is always in union with *Brahman*; he is neither overexcited to receive pleasant news nor weeps on hearing unpleasant tidings. Contacts with the outer world will not create turmoil in the mind of such a person. He finds permanent happiness in his *atman* by remaining engaged in meditation on the Supreme. He is convinced that the pleasures of the world are impermanent and therefore produce grief. Absolute freedom is the goal; it can be achieved by abandoning dualities, practising self-control and working for the welfare of creation.

Krishna now touches the fringe of Dhyana Yoga or meditation. By concentration of the mind on a point, cutting off all contacts with the outside world, regulating the rhythm of breathing, controlling the senses, thoughts and intellect, surrendering them to the Supreme, freeing the self from desires, fear and anger, one may achieve liberation.

Thus, thoughtful and balanced actions ultimately merge into renunciation and meditation.

This is the essence of the fifth chapter of the *Gita*, entitled *The Yoga of Renunciation of Action.*

Action and renunciation are two faces of the same coin. But relinquishing inner conflicts is essential for complete liberation, action being the primary step in the journey. By performance, you exhaust your *vaasnas* (subtle tendencies) and tame your desires. Otherwise one cannot prevent revolting desires from accumulating more and more foolishly. So, succeed you must in materialistic achievements but through an intelligent approach. Performance for worldly fulfilment with a detached attitude towards the outcome makes the ego a friendly supporter. Your mind becomes calm and suitable for further contemplation and, ultimately, the Yoga of Renunciation is achieved through wise actions.

Live a full life; watch the game of desires and ego; be poised and balanced and believe in the arrangement of Nature. One single phenomenon pervades all living, non-living and even non-existent systems; help them evolve and express themselves. Be in union with Omnipresent Consciousness. Living a complete life in all respects does not perturb the one who is fixed in Yoga – in a unity of the Self and the Supreme. Distress will come and go; happiness will come and go; all are finite. But if plugged with the Infinite, peace will prevail infinitely.

Absolute Freedom and stability in the fearless, composed mind is the goal of life, even while working and enjoying the world. This must be achieved for fulfilment. Such a state can be reached by the practice of meditation, regular retrospection, contributing to the welfare of all creation –

particularly the have-nots, the destitute and the environment. Surrender your being at the altar of the Supreme and be liberated.

Gita Gyana 5

- ❑ **5.1:** Action is superior to relinquishment of action.
- ❑ **5.2:** Intelligently performed action will lead to negation of conflicts in the mind.
- ❑ **5.3:** Have no extreme likes or dislikes. They create contradiction within the mind.
- ❑ **5.4:** The mind purified through detached action becomes capable of contemplation. Rejection of wild desires is a must before purification.
- ❑ **5.5:** Don't let the ego become inflated by your high achievements. Watch out!
- ❑ **5.6:** Realise that the whole drama of the universe, including that of your life, is directed by Nature.
- ❑ **5.7:** The *atman* – Pure Consciousness within us – is the Observer. Only our mind is involved in happiness and unhappiness and the ego suffers the pangs of both.
- ❑ **5.8:** To remove your sufferings, unveil the knowledge by destroying ignorance about the Self.
- ❑ **5.9:** Be equipoised and cultivate unshakable wisdom to reach the Reality.
- ❑ **6.0:** Practice of meditation, self-analysis, kindness towards the needy and abandoning wild desires shall liberate you – free you from nerve-shattering anxiety, problems and unhappiness.

5. Action roasts the seeds of *vaasnas*. Renunciation roasts the seeds of action. Act and renounce desires! *Karma* will not germinate.

Chapter 6

Meditation: The Quietude of Mind

Krishna's assertion implies that withdrawal of actions is only concerned a little with the outer world. It is mainly an attitude of mind and intellect. Actually, the Yoga of Action, or disciplined activity, without craving and anxiety for its fruits, is the real renunciation. No one becomes a renunciate if he does not reject selfish tendencies as well as self-gratification. Action is a means to the advent of Yoga; then the resultant serenity, achieved in Yoga, further becomes a means to reach the unfolding Self. A man is free to decide and act for ameliorating or deteriorating his circumstances. One has to take full responsibility for oneself. If we abandon selfish desires, channelling our thoughts in the right direction, our 'self' supports us as a friend; otherwise it may act as a foe. At the level of the body (comfort-discomfort), the mind (life-death), and intellect (honour-dishonour), the pairs of opposite eventualities do not agitate the mind of a wise man.

Krishna continues to enumerate the characteristics of a yogi (a person in union with the Self): one who is content with knowledge and wisdom (i.e., not dreaming of wealth, power or fame), firm (in values), not greedy, and even-minded amongst fair, neutral or evil persons, becomes outstandingly proficient.

Introducing the teaching of meditation, Krishna says that the yogi should try to be alert constantly and concentrate his mind on the Supreme; he should try to live in solitude (i.e., having withdrawn senses, thoughts, and reasoning) and be free from the agitation of yearnings.

Eternal peace dwells within us, not without, hence a yogi (practising meditation) should first shun outer stimuli at the body, mind, intellect and ego levels, bringing the self to a standstill without a single ripple of anxiety. He should sit on a clean, firm seat that is neither too high nor too low and moderately soft and comfortable, and make the mind single-pointed. This preparatory method should purify his internal being. He should keep his body erect (while sitting) with head and neck (and the trunk) in a straight posture (perpendicular to the cross-folded lower limbs in the sitting position and putting both hands on his lap); he should (mentally) look at the tip of his nose (or at the centre of the two eyebrows; eyes partially or completely closed), without letting the eyes wander around.

On this threshold of *dhyana*, the mind of the seeker should be serene, self-controlled in all aspects of thinking, including sensuous impulse, and contemplate the Supreme (or a symbol, sound, concept, or a personal or impersonal God – super-imposed by faith in the Supreme). Thus the yogi who is equi-balanced finds perfect peace, which is the nature of Consciousness.

However, for one who eats too much or too little (and seldom), and who sleeps too much or often keeps awake, Yoga is not attainable. This means a balanced, disciplined, regulated and moderate (without excesses) way of life is the most suited approach for yogic practice. Freedom from the clutches of (wild) desires, regulation of the mind and anchorage in the Self leads one to be connected with the Supreme through Yoga. This is an experience that transcends all knowledge. This experience is unique and beyond description – the thoughts are silent, the Supreme Self illumining the Inner Self, the achievement is par excellence. After reaching That, one is not shattered even in the greatest grief. A firm determination for continual practice is required for gaining unshakable quietude – even if at a slow pace of progress. The mind often runs wild but the yogi brings it back to the altar of the Supreme wherein lies Infinite Bliss. When the yogi thus attains union with the Divine, he becomes one with the cosmos. He 'sees' Him in all phenomena. Even while performing actions in the world, such a wise man adores the Self in oneness with all beings and looks at every episode, happy or unhappy, with unperturbed equanimity.

Being an intelligent young prince, Arjuna doubts the achievement of permanency in the dispassion of the mind. He, therefore, admits to Krishna that the mind is restless, adamant, strong and boisterous to be brought under control. This reasoning sounds valid. On hearing this, Krishna answers that certainly the mind is restless and revolting, hence Yoga is hard to accomplish, but by self-control and practice through proper means, success crowns the seeker. Besides, even if one fails in spite of sincere efforts, he is a sure recipient for Grace from the Supreme, Who blesses him to take wings on the evolutionary path through later developments in spirituality as well as the quality of life. Thereupon, by persistently striving hard for perfection, one reaches the ultimate goal, passing through the vicissitudes of Time.

Krishna further adds that a realised yogi is better than the *sannyasi* (renunciate) who abandons performance; the yogi is also greater than the man of knowledge (concerning only religion, rituals and worldly affairs), and the ritualist (who performs rituals). Therefore, Krishna advises Arjuna to become a yogi.

This is the essence of the sixth chapter of the *Gita*, entitled *The Yoga of Meditation*.

The quietude of mind can be attained by several techniques that have been laid down from time to time in all the faiths of the world. In this discourse, Yogiraj Krishna initiates Arjuna into the salient features of Dhyana Yoga (meditation) – the ultimate immanence in all components of Yoga.

The science of meditation has been a popular subject amongst the learned through millennia for interpretation, research, commentary, moderation to suit the changing times, analysis, synthesis, and innovation.

In the *Gita*, Krishna narrates this unfathomable subject only by indicative points. The ever-new unfolding of these directives reveals an inexhaustible treasure of wisdom. Therefore, keeping in view the need of the present-day seeker, who requires time-saving, cut-and-dried techniques, an Appendix on Dhyana Yoga (meditation) is given at the end of this book. The core is based on the concept taught by Yogiraj Krishna, yet some interpretations contributed by the learned over time have been added, which may answer some of the common questions a seeker asks. Such variations and moderations incorporated here may assist the beginner.

To be receptive to the positivity of Yoga and to absorb its intensively glowing experience, one has to cleanse the clutter in his mind. The yogi changes his attitude and thought pattern by detachment and discrimination while acting in the world; he rejects selfishness and feels enriched by wisdom alone. He must develop equanimity of mind towards all situations and persons; also, he must have unshakable faith in the Omnipresent Consciousness. This structure of thought and behaviour develops only by constant contemplation within and a vigorous awareness outside while performing. Also, if one acquires quietude of mind and the right method of thinking, one reaches the top of the ladder of success in whatever field of activity he is engaged in. Even for social recognition, material gains, sense of fulfilment and peace, such a purification of the mind is a prerequisite. One must try hard to conquer greed, an unfruitful mind agitated by pleasant and unpleasant experiences, and doubts about the timeless unity of Creation.

The concentration of mind (or annihilation of thoughts by rigorously observing them), albeit apparently difficult, is the key to meditation. Single-pointed focusing of the mind can be achieved by unplugging it from endless desires and by continuous practice. At regular moments of suitable duration, solitude, a comfortable sitting posture, rhythmic breathing, without contact with the outside world through the body, eyes, mind, or otherwise, focusing attention on a personal God (with form) or impersonal (Pure Consciousness, Truth, Reality, having no attributes or form; or whatever one conceives according to his convictions), and surrendering the ego to the Self shall bring forth a dissolution of one's 'existence' into the experience of peace.

When one comes out of this bliss, one feels a calmness that takes him to higher planes for effective and balanced action in the world outside. The success in Yoga depends on how disciplined and moderate one is in eating, sleeping, worldly relations and the dissipation of vital energy in futile exercises.

This transcendental experience is unparalleled, can never be procured by wealth, power or control over worldly systems. Repeatedly, one has to bring back the wandering mind and focus it with patience and perseverance. Ultimately, the seeker merges with the Silence of the Universe and unites permanently with Him. Then he may act with all his vigour outside in the world. No situation, whatsoever, can shake him. He achieves perfection in all aspects of his personality.

Gita Gyana 6

- ❑ **6.1:** Detachment is an attitude of mind, not cessation of work.
- ❑ **6.2:** Renounce selfish tendencies of the mind to attain peace.
- ❑ **6.3:** You are yourself responsible for your development or retardation.
- ❑ **6.4:** Do not be agitated by pairs of opposite experiences – pleasant or unpleasant – in life that arise repeatedly.

- 6.5: Be firm, without greed, and even-minded in all walks of life.
- 6.6: Meditation is the key to succeed and to evolve.
- 6.7: Clean your Inner Self from the clutter of fantasies and boisterous desires.
- 6.8: During certain times in the day, sit comfortably, close your eyes, then concentrate on the Eternal Phenomenon, and tame wandering thoughts by withdrawal and practice.
- 6.9: Contemplate through Yoga, and act through a serene, purified, compassionate mind.
- 7.0: Thus, achieve worldly success as well as union with the Truth by way of Yoga.

> **6. All epoch-making contributions in the world are the product of minds in deep meditation!**

Chapter 7

The Insight of Illusion: Gateway to Freedom

In order to elucidate how the finite intelligence of man can comprehend the Infinite Reality, Krishna deals here with the nature of the Truth, the World and the Divine Illusion. He says that when the unmanifested Nature (*prakriti*) of Pure Consciousness manifests, It takes the form of earth, water, fire, air, ether, mind, intellect and egoism. This eight-fold creation is the lower nature of the Lord while the higher nature comprises the life-factor (soul), which supports this world. Thus, God includes in entirety the Unconscious of His lower nature and the Conscious of His higher nature. Krishna asserts that all beings originate from these two natures and so also the world disintegrates and disperses back in them. That means, God includes the universe within Himself, projects it from His own nature and takes it back into Himself.

The state of being and the immanence of the essence (*dharma*) of all animates and inanimates are the expressions of Pure Consciousness; for example, He is the taste in water, light in the moon and the sun, the syllable AUM in all the *Vedas*, sound in ether, virility in man, and so on. Further, all the vital and glorious capabilities like intelligence in the intelligent, splendour in the splendid, righteous desire in the pure being, etc, shine forth from His expression.

The three states of basic qualities in persons – the *sattvic* (harmonious, pure, detached mind), *rajasic* (passionate activity), and *tamasic* (inactivity, reluctance to exert oneself; inertness) – are all from Him but He is not in them. The world functions within these threefold predominating attitudes or qualities (*gunas*) which form the Divine *Maya* (or illusion). But this *maya*, manipulating the three *gunas*, is normally not recognised by the world. He, the Absolute, is above these *gunas*, and the one who takes refuge in Him crosses over from *maya* (fallacy of illusion).

Krishna further states that evildoers are fools because their minds are covered by illusion; they do not surrender (their ego) to the Almighty. From amongst the virtuous ones, he who is single-minded and constantly in union with the Divine will attain Him. The ignorant imposes shape and quality on the Formless Reality because he does not comprehend that the Reality is without any form and attributes. It is Changeless and Supreme. His real nature is hidden behind the Creative Power, which fact only a few can realise. Thus, the utterly confused world does not know the Unborn and the Unchanging.

The Supreme knows the past, the present and the future but no one knows Him. All beings live under the awe of delusion, as they are victims of dual experiences, desires and hate. But those who are virtuous and liberated from the mistaken belief of contradictions in life are steadfast in the service of the Divine. Those who surrender at the altar of Pure Consciousness make great efforts for becoming free from the agony of old age and death. They know *Brahman* (the Absolute), the Self and the Action.

Only he who has cultivated a balanced mind and a firm faith in the Almighty all through his life, remains fixed in the knowledge of the Truth, even at the time of death.

This is the essence of the seventh chapter of the *Gita*, entitled *The Yoga of Wisdom and Knowledge*.

Modern astronomy and theoretical physics are heading towards the conclusion that the Universe and Time were created with the Big Bang. Since then, some 14 billion years ago, the universe is expanding with a speed more than that of light. Therefore, as per the present time, we cannot 'observe' or calculate the 'boundary' of the Universe because no device can overtake the speed of light. The initial momentum of the Big Bang is acting ever faster. However, it has been calculated that in the distant future this acceleration will be exhausted and the universe will start collapsing back on itself until it will be reduced to a tiny Black Hole – an extremely dense body with infinite density, infinite gravitational force and infinite mass from which even light cannot escape.

What a striking similarity in concept with the *Gita*! Yogiraj Krishna says that the universe originates from *Brahman* (the Absolute), remains in Him and is ultimately absorbed into *Brahman*. To have an insight of the illusion, it must be clearly understood that all the gross elements and the mind, intelligence, ego and the life-factor are born from Pure Consciousness. They are, however, unreal because they take birth and they die. How can they be the Truth and Reality if they disintegrate and vanish? Hence, only the Supreme is Real because it is Unborn and Imperishable. All are from Him but He is from none.

His *maya* is a great power – the Divine Illusion, under the influence of which the Inner Self forgets its real nature, i.e., Bliss (*ananda*), which is nothing but the Absolute. Thus, the self, covered with *maya*, behaves as ego, and the ego suffers.

Nothing is higher than God-perfect. All vital and glorious qualities in beings and in Nature are His expressions. The illusion plays through the three types of predominant qualities of beings – *harmonious*, *passionate*, and *inert*. The sloths are inactive and the performers with attachment are passionately hyperactive. The balanced, compassionate, unattached being, however, may know Him but ultimately this quality has also to be imbibed within to reach Him in union. Such a person, very close to Pure Consciousness, is the recipient of His Grace.

The worldly accumulation of wealth, power or fame is not negated here but it must not be forgotten that they are unstable. Multiple faiths in various deities, paths or preachers may yield temporary benefits but single-minded adherence to the One Absolute is the best way, which brings permanent happiness, peace, and salvation. Leave hate and fear; do not allow favourable and unfavourable situations to overcome and upset you; act without selfish passion and agitation in mind; such a state can be achieved only when you always experience His presence within yourself.

Old age is very troublesome, with all its dissipating conditions of the body and a plethora of ailments. Above all, the greatest agony of old age is the fear of death. Death itself may not be painful but it is horrifying if one has not developed a positive attitude towards it. Such an attitude cannot be cultivated in a day or two; it is a lifetime's undertaking. The total sum of qualities of your humane thoughts, good actions, harmony in life, positive comprehension of life and the Divine, and an unshakable faith in the Almighty, which you have earned by right living, sustains your knowledge of the Truth even at the time of departure from this world.

Thus, the natural process of transformation from this life to another plane of existence becomes serene and facile.

Gita Gyana 7

- ❑ **7.1:** The man with finite intelligence can comprehend Infinite Reality by an insight of the Divine Illusion.
- ❑ **7.2:** When the unexpressed Nature of Pure Consciousness manifests, the universe is created.
- ❑ **7.3:** The universe originates from, sustains on, and dissolves in the Nature of the Absolute Self.
- ❑ **7.4:** The essence of qualities in living and non-living beings is the expression of the All-pervading Self.
- ❑ **7.5:** The glorious capabilities and talents of beings are, all the more, vital expressions of the Almighty.

- **7.6:** One should abandon *reluctance to exert oneself* (*tamas*), so as to achieve the state of *passionate activity* (*rajas*); in due course, however, *rajas* is also to be left behind in order to reach a *harmonious, compassionate, pure state of life* (*sattvic*).
- **7.7:** The illusion functions through the above-cited three states in beings; therefore, one must try hard to get out of all the three to achieve complete liberation.
- **7.8:** Lay your ego before Him and do not impose limited forms on the Limitless and the Formless Reality.
- **7.9:** The past, present and future are known to the God-Principle; so, why worry?
- **8.0:** The sum total of purity of your mind, thoughts, actions and love, which accrue during your lifetime, maintains your knowledge about the Truth even at the deathbed and helps make an agonyless journey of transformation to the other plane of time.

> **7. Divine Illusion can be removed only by Divine Grace, which can come only when you are in union with the Divine.**

Chapter 8

Get in Touch with the Self: The Eternal Truth

Entering into deeper aspects of the cosmic structure, Arjuna's inquisitiveness now focuses on some pertinent questions: What is *Brahman* (the Absolute)? What is the Self? What is *karma*? And what are the regions of elements (perishable existence) and the gods (possessor of special faculty)? What is the essential sacrifice in the body? How shall a self-controlled being know the Divine at the time of death?

To these penetrating questions, Krishna answers authoritatively:

Brahman is the Absolute, which is Indestructible.

It becomes the Self as Spirit, illuminating all functions in man and Nature.

Karma is the creative instinct and power from which the entire cosmos evolved.

The Personal God (*Ishwara*) is the Cosmic Lord -- the object of all devotion, while the Immutable Divine, Absolute, the Impersonal God (*Brahman*) is the Supra-cosmic Reality, a Presiding Deity of the Cosmos, and above all.

All created Nature is mutable or perishable.

The basis for all essential sacrifices is knowledge of the Self.

The *jiva* is the individual soul which shares some qualities of the Divine as well.

In short, the Absolute (*Brahman*) alone is Real and all else is a superimposition upon it.

Krishna explains further that one who remembers the Divine at the time of death, reaches the Eternal. Therefore, Krishna advises Arjuna to be consistently in mental contact with the Eternal and to perform proper actions in the world. Thus, he who meditates throughout his life on the Supreme Being by regular practice with single-pointed concentration realises the Supreme Being – the Greatest, the Subtlest, and the Brightest of all. At the time of his departure from this world, with unwavering mind, devotion and steady Yoga of meditation, if one sets his thoughts in the centre of the eyebrows and lays down his life before the Supreme, he attains the Divine Being.

Also, one who utters the single-syllabled AUM, which is *Brahman*, remembering Him, leaves this body and becomes one with the Absolute. AUM is the sound-symbol of the Absolute. It denotes the expression of the Divine when His manifestation begins.

Ever-disciplined yogis reach the Divine easily, and from there they don't come back to the realm of sorrows and sufferings. Else, all worlds, including Brahmaji, are subject to rebirth, circling in the cycles of existence and non-existence.

Elaborating further on the structure of the cosmos, Krishna says that one day of Brahmaji is of a thousand *Yugas* (ages, aeon, a long period of time) long and so also his night, alternating with the day. The day represents cosmic manifestation (expression of the Absolute) and the night indicates non-manifestation. With the coming of day, all is manifested from the unmanifested Absolute, and with the advent of night, all is again dissolved in the unmanifested. This process repeats itself again and again and the same arrays of existence and beings are born in recurrence, then helplessly merge into the unmanifested with the onset of night.

But beyond and above this manifested and unmanifested states, there exists yet another Unmanifested Eternal Being who does not perish even when all is dissolved. That is the Highest Goal (status, intent, or plane) from where the achiever does not come back. By union with Him, the seeker's wholeness of conscious being becomes complete. That Highest Terminus, the Supreme Abode of *Ishwara* (the Personal God), is *Para-Brahma*, the Absolute. This is the *Uttam Purusha* (the Supreme Person) in Whom all creation exists and Who pervades everything. He, however, is attainable by unshakable devotion.

Krishna reveals the time connotation in which a yogi leaving his body does not return, and also that time when a departing yogi must return. If a yogi with knowledge of *Brahman* leaves the body in the presence of fire, light, daytime, that half of the month when the moon shines, and the six months of the year when the path of the sun is inclined northwards, he goes to the Absolute, and does not return. On the other hand, if a yogi departs in the presence of smoke, night, the dark-half of the month, and six months of the year when the path of the sun is south-inclined, he obtains the plane of moonlight (a pure and peaceful state of existence) but from where he is bound to return. These two aspects represent a contrast between the light and darkness. Knowledge is the path of light and ignorance is the path of darkness; so are liberation and bondage, respectively.

The yogi who knows these paths, who discretely follows the way of knowledge rather than that of ignorance, never goes astray. Therefore, Krishna tells Arjuna to be firm in Yoga. The yogi is well established in thoughts of the Eternal; he has no attachment with the fruits of his performance; thus he attains the Supreme, the Original and the Real Nature of himself.

This is the essence of the eighth chapter of the *Gita*, entitled *The Yoga of the Imperishable Absolute*.

The structure and functional organisation of the universe is self-generative as well as self-dissolving in a cyclic manner. However, the Absolute (*Brahman*) is Indestructible. It is the Reality beyond cycles of the cosmos. The Spirit is the expression of the Absolute in all entities as the Self. *Karma* is the force that makes the cosmos evolve and also urges beings to act and perform. We love and offer our devotion to *Ishwara* (Personal God). It could be an idol, a cross, a crescent, a book, an object, a crown, a flag, a concept, a word or any other sign of one's choice or faith. By faith and devotion the Lord of Cosmic Existence (*Ishwara*) expresses Himself through forms and shapes.

On the other hand, the Impersonal God (*Para-Brahma*, the Absolute) is a Formless, Shapeless, Timeless, and Spaceless Supra-cosmic Reality that presides over the cosmos. All others constitute the infra-status with relation to the Absolute.

The *jiva* (ego) is the individual soul veiled by ignorance; the *jiva* has some attributes of the Divine as well as Nature, yet it suffers the agony produced by *karma* because it is engulfed by illusion. The moment it rediscovers itself as being a part and parcel of the Supreme, by removal of the veil of ignorance, suffering vanishes and the *jiva* is liberated.

In order to conquer the agony of old age and death, one must practise devotion, meditation, virtuous deeds and walk on righteous paths throughout life. Meditation on the Supreme (Expressed or Absolute) on one's deathbed makes the transition to the other plane an easy process. But unless such practice is done throughout life, it is improbable to fix the mind on the Divine at the last moment of life.

Lord Krishna clearly emphasises that pronouncing or remembering the single-syllabled AUM at the time of death liberates the person. It is a vibrating, long-resounding sound symbolising the process of Generation, Orchestration and Dissolution (GOD), and also beyond that – the Eternity. It has no religious connotation of any particular faith; instead, it is the power point of all creation, existence and absorption reflected from the Immutable. Remembering AUM encompasses an awareness of the whole cosmos and its faultless evolution, which operates at the will of the Highest Intelligence.

The creation and dissolution of the universe is a cyclic process. The Cosmic Intelligence is, however, above and beyond this cycle. It is the Absolute that only observes the great phenomenon of evolution and dissolution of the cosmos.

The path of light, i.e., knowledge, takes the wise beyond this cycle, but the path of darkness, i.e., ignorance, binds the unwise in the bondage of illusion. Therefore, one must be in meditation, contemplation and concentration on the Supreme and one must walk on the path of light to be rid of the illusion of happiness and unhappiness in this world.

Gita Gyana 8

- **8.1:** *Brahman* is the Absolute. It is above and beyond all, Indestructible and Omnipresent. It is also known as an Impersonal God.
- **8.2:** *Ishwara* is the Personal God, the Supreme. It is the Lord of the Cosmos. Its Abode is in the Absolute. It is the object of all devotion.
- **8.3:** The Supreme expresses Itself as 'Self' (soul) in all beings as well as in Nature. It illumines all functions and qualities.
- **8.4:** The *jiva* is the reflection of the individual soul. It shares the attributes of the Divine as well as Nature. But it forgets its own blissful nature under the veil of ignorance and illusion, and hence acts as ego and suffers pains and pleasures of the world.
- **8.5:** Thus, *Brahman* alone is Real and the rest are a superimposition upon it.
- **8.6:** If one practises remembering the Almighty, meditating upon Him throughout life, then only

could one remember Him at the time of death. Thereafter, one does not re-enter the realm of agony, sorrow and conflicts, and achieves a calm, non-fearing transformation into the other plane of existence.

- ❑ **8.7:** The goal of our life is to achieve complete happiness. This lies with the Supreme, so one has to attune oneself with Him to get rid of pain.
- ❑ **8.8:** The right path takes us to that goal. The wrong path takes us to repeated unhappiness and mental torture. A positive, pure and compassionate attitude creates the right path.
- ❑ **8.9:** The wise man can distinguish between the path of light (knowledge) and that of darkness (ignorance).
- ❑ **9.0:** You are the Self within you; that is the expression of *Brahman*. Discover yourself and live a completely happy life, full of vigour and action.

8. Our pure intellect is in the proximity of the Absolute, a ray of which is reflected in it, at times – and a miracle is born!

Chapter 9

The Fire of Awareness

Unabated Grace showers on Arjuna as Krishna promises to reveal the secret of conceptual wisdom – the philosophy of Truth as well as practical knowledge to achieve that wisdom. This profundity could as well be imbibed and verified by direct experience.

Krishna continues that Pure Consciousness pervades this universe through the unmanifested form of the Supreme. All beings exist in the Supreme but He does not make His dwelling in them. It is a Divine Mystery that the Spirit (His reflection) sustains beings but does not make a place of living in them. All beings are absorbed back by Nature at the end of the Cosmic Cycle, and are created again by Him at the beginning of the next cycle. Helplessly, worldly beings come and go recurrently through such cycles.

Krishna says that under the guidance of the Supreme, moving and non-moving things are born from Nature (*prakriti*), and the wheel of existence rotates on. Misled ones do not realise His real nature. They indulge in acts of cruelty and greed, without discernment. On the other hand, realised ones remain in the Divine nature, and with an unshakable belief they know Him as the source of all existence, surrendering unto Him with intense devotion.

The Lord Himself represents all actions, all components and all results of worship, sacrifice and rituals. He Himself is each and every conceivable phenomenon in the universe. He is also the Eternal Seed of all, and is Imperishable.

Those learned men who perform religious rituals with prayer and sacrifice (service) putting labour and pious intentions, may gain temporary heavenly enjoyment in the futuristic plane, yet they do not reach the goal of union with the Supreme; thus, they have to return in the cycle of birth and death, and happiness and unhappiness because they perspire with egocentric desires of reaching the heavenly state only.

Instead, those who meditate on the Supreme alone and worship Him with single-minded perseverance (without the desire for heavenly enjoyment) shall receive fulfilment of all that which they do not have and so also protection of what they have. This implies that the Lord shall confer upon them His Grace and shall also provide security for that achievement. However, devotion of all kinds to varied powers of lesser or higher stature brings varied results, but the lesser one brings lesser rewards and the highest one brings the Highest Grace.

Krishna says that He accepts all offerings made with love, devotion and a pure heart – be it a leaf, a flower, a fruit, or water. It means that wealth and ostentation do not play any role in the worship of God; it is love and devotion that matters. Also, whatever routine task one does – working, eating, offering donations, observing austerity, etc – should be done as a self-offering to the Lord. By such practice, one becomes free from the bond of actions, i.e., the actions do not generate *karma,* and one is liberated from good or bad results of actions. The mind should be firm on relinquishment to acquire freedom and attain Him.

Krishna continues to throw light on the relationship between God and worldly beings. He says that He is in all beings. None is hateful or endearing to Him. But those who adore Him with devotion are in His heart and He is in theirs – they are very dear to Him. Krishna asserts that even if a person is morally low and deplorable but worships the Supreme with unwavering mind and pure devotion, he must be considered righteous because he has taken the right path of devotion. Such a being will soon be purified and attain peace. Krishna reveals that a devotee of God never perishes.

Irrespective of caste, creed, learning (of worldly affairs), gender or status, those who take refuge in the Almighty attain the highest goal. No distinction of any sort has been allowed in achieving salvation. All are one in the eyes of the Almighty. The path is easier for those who are rightly and conveniently placed in life and possess an aptitude for worship, devotion and spirituality.

Krishna concludes here that realisation of the Supreme should be the goal of life for all beings and hence be fulfilled by reaching Him; this could be successfully done by fixing the mind on Him and by steadfastly worshipping Him. In this way, discipline will set into one's life and through reverence one could reach the goal.

This is the essence of the ninth chapter of the *Gita,* entitled *The Yoga of Royal Knowledge and Royal Secret.*

The secret of experiencing the Divine, the right relationship with the world, success in life, and adjustment of attitudes towards adversities has been disclosed here. Such knowledge can be verified and comprehended by direct experience, but faith in the very essence is important; otherwise one cannot get out of conflicts.

The universe is because of Absolute Reality but He is far above the universe. The ego (the soul covered with ignorance) is the receiver and enjoyer of *karma*. If the ego is disciplined on the right path, *karma* does not generate fruits – good or bad. The Self is thus liberated. In other words, if the ego is not there to suffer, how can we suffer?

It is *prakriti* (Nature) that makes the universe function. Man is only a component in the whole system through whom Pure Consciousness is expressed. So, the inner reality in all things is He whom we are unable to recognise normally. All animates and inanimates have the same spark of the Supreme. No one should be rated high or low by way of birth, wealth, intelligence, power, positioning or influence of any sort.

Involvement in the act of unrighteous nature, ruthlessness, greed, and wild desires develop agitation and a confused state of non-understanding. Consequently, one cannot identify the underlying Reality and gets entangled in worldly contradictions and grief.

Therefore, knowledge and awareness about the Reality of the universe and Nature, dedicated devotion, discipline, and skilful work lead to the highest perfection. Take refuge in Him and surrender everything unto Him; by the laying down of ego, one does not develop yearning for unstable sense gratification. The goal of attaining Imperishable Bliss may thus be fulfilled.

If we do work with a sense of offering to the Giver, our act turns into compassion, sympathy, help for destitute beings, and support for the environment (inanimates), uplift of the downtrodden, altruism and cooperation with creation. Otherwise, how else are we to make our offerings to Him? Rituals are of little consequence and you cannot meet Him in person to make offerings!

Everyone has a right to worship and achieve liberation. The question of high or low in any sense does not arise. All are equal in His eyes; therefore, we must not take a partisan view in any case of positioning or difference in faiths.

The essential ingredient to achieve perfection encompasses meditation, courage, steadfastness of character, the right path in keeping the body and mind healthy, and a firm belief in His scheme of things that we cannot change. All these together make a man perfect.

Gita Gyana 9

- ❑ **9.1:** Transcendental wisdom, practical knowledge of experiencing the Divine and rational functioning in the world free us from sorrow.

- ❑ **9.2:** Look at the world with equanimity because all beings as well as Nature are sustained by one single Power.
- ❑ **9.3:** Throughout Cosmic Time, the cycles of creation and dissolution go on incessantly. Then why lament over the perishable?
- ❑ **9.4:** The Eternal, the Supreme, is an Observer, unaffected by happenings and unattached to anything. Only his *prakriti* puts forth this show.
- ❑ **9.5:** Symbolised powers could be the path to reach the goal, but they are not the goal in themselves, which is above and beyond all conceptualised things, forms and shapes.
- ❑ **9.6:** To rediscover one's total identity with the Self, one must glorify the Lord, strive hard, surrender and be stable in pursuit of the goal.
- ❑ **9.7:** Banish dogmatic rituals, feeling high or low, and egocentric arrogance in achievements of worldly pleasures. One must not look down upon low-placed beings because the Grace of the Almighty illumines them also.
- ❑ **9.8:** The entire creation is intimately interconnected and He is present everywhere, being the Master of all.
- ❑ **9.9:** Don't compromise with smaller achievements and temporary happiness or else you will return again and again. Aim high and achieve freedom.
- ❑ **10.0:** Constant awareness, contemplation on the Self (meditation), a positive attitude, and righteous acts are the secret of success.

> **9. We make the path our goal – we suffer! We make the goal our path – we suffer! Cross over both, the path and the goal, only then will an Unknowable Goal be created before you!**

Chapter 10

Divine Glories Empower Meditation

So far, Arjuna is delighted to hear Krishna's teachings, so Krishna willingly continues to impart the Supreme Knowledge to him. Krishna says that the origin of the Supreme is not known even to the gods, or to the great sages because He is the cause of their origin itself.

Krishna asserts that different characteristics of beings permeate through the Supreme alone; such qualities and conditions are: intelligence, knowledge, non-enchantment, patience, truth, self-control, and calmness, happiness and unhappiness, birth and death, fear and fearlessness, non-violence, equipoise, contentment, austerity, charity, fame and the condition of being infamous.

The Seven Great Sages and the Ancient Four, as well as Manu (first amongst men), are also of the nature of the Supreme. They were born from the mind of the Supreme and from them the beings of the world originated. These primordial manifestations of the Supreme could as well be understood as primary levels of energy responsible for the advent of various processes in the universe. They are our fields of experience at the body, mind, intellect and ego level through which the world of the superpower is projected. Thus, one who knows the multiple manifestations of the Supreme (His Glory), as well as His Power (Yoga), attains steadfastness in unquivering Yoga.

Those who know that the Supreme is the origin of all shall worship Him with love and live in harmony with creation. Such beings will attain the bliss of remaining in the true state of Pure Consciousness.

Krishna was in the State of the Supreme and this wisdom was being expressed directly through Him. Therefore, on hearing all this, Arjuna accepts all that is told to him, and submits to Krishna that He (Krishna, the Expression of the Absolute) was the Supreme *Brahman*, Supreme Abode, Supreme Purifier, the Eternal, Divine Person, the First of Gods, Unborn, the All-pervading. Arjuna adds that such declarations of wisdom have been made earlier by great sages also, and now he has heard it from Krishna Himself who is in the State of Absolute Being. All that was told to him convinces Arjuna but his thirst for knowledge is not yet quenched. He, therefore, wants to hear from Krishna the specific aspects in creation that he can 'see' and comprehend therein the manifestation of the Lord more vividly.

Although every particle in the state of existence or non-existence expresses the nature of the Supreme and there is no end to the extent of the Divine presence, there are certain aspects in which His glory and magnificence are manifested more prominently. In order to satisfy the curiosity of Arjuna, Krishna narrates only few such examples where He is projected magnificently.

Krishna says that amongst the *Adityas* (gods) He is Vishnu – the sustainer of creation; of Light, He is the Sun – the prime source of energy; of the wind and breeze aspect (*Maruts*), He is Marichi – the chief. Of all illuminations of the night, He is expressed most in the Moon (beatitude and serenity).

Of the *Vedas*, He is the *Sama Veda* (with musical excellence); of gods, He is Indra (the highest achiever); of the body, He is expressed most in the Mind (the most powerful equipment which, if properly channelled, could achieve the Supreme); of beings with all grosser faculties, He is Consciousness (the subtlest of all).

Krishna further indicates that from amongst the custodians of various planes of powers, He is the one in whom the Supreme is manifested with the highest degree: of *Rudras* – He is *Sankara* (Shiva – the Annihilator); of the *Yaksas* and *Raksas* – He is Kubera (the Treasurer of heavenly treasures); of *Vaasus* – He is Agni (Fire); of Mountain Peaks – He is Meru; of Gurus – He is Brahaspati (the Guru of Gods); of military chieftains – He is Skanda (the Powerful Warrior); of Water Bodies – He is the Ocean.

Continuing, Krishna says that the Supreme is best expressed in Sage Bhragu amongst the great sages; AUM in sounds; Meditation in offerings; and Himalaya in the immobiles; the Peepal tree (*Ficus religiosa*) in trees; Narada (the great devotee of Vishnu) in Divine Seers; Chitraratha in *Gandharvas* (heavenly dancers and musicians); Sage Kapila (propounder of Sankhya Yoga) in those who attain perfection.

The Supreme is best revealed in Uchaisravas (the heavenly horse obtained from *Samundra Manthan* – churning of the sea by gods and demons), of horses; so also Airavata, of lordly elephants; and the King amongst men; *Vajra* the most powerful weapon producing thunder-lightning, created from the bones of the ribcage of Rishi Dadhichi – for the use of Indra (the chief of gods against the demons), amongst the armours.

Kamdhenu (the heavenly cow with desire-fulfilling power) of the cows; *Kamadeva* (the god of love and virility) of the Procreators; *Vasuki* (the celestial, small but powerful serpent who decorates Lord Shiva's little finger) of the serpents.

Citing outstanding examples of the revelation of Supreme characterisations, Krishna continues to enumerate that He is the *Anant Naga* (the lordly, hooded snake-god who serves as a reclining cushion for Lord Vishnu) of the Nagas; *Varuna* – god of the inhabitants of the water; *Aryama* of the Pitras (ancestors); Lord *Yama* (King of Death), amongst the authoritarian to maintain law and order; *Prahalada* (a great devotee of Lord Vishnu with human perfection) of the giant race; Time of those who count and calculate; Lion of beasts; mighty *Garuda* (the flying carrier-bird-god serving Lord Vishnu) of birds.

The Supreme is revealed most prominently in the wind amongst purifiers; in Lord *Rama*, amongst combatants; in the crocodile, amongst fish (meaning the creatures that live in water); and the Ganges (the holiest river), amongst rivers.

The Supreme Himself is the beginning, the middle and the end in the process of creation; the Science of the Self (which uncovers the wisdom from ignorance and identifies our true nature in Pure Consciousness), of all the sciences; the logic amongst debaters; the letter 'A', amongst letters (denoting the origin; it is the first letter of all languages of the world); the pair of words (dual – which coordinate each other), amongst all compounds (words).

The Supreme is Imperishable Time and also the Creator, the Omniscient. He is fame, prosperity, speech, memory, intelligence, firmness, and patience in feminine being – implying thereby that wherever these qualities are revealed more eminently in a female, the expression of the Lord is visible. He represents the *Gayatri Mantra* amongst mantras (Gayatri metre being the prayer of light and wisdom). He is also manifested more in the *Margashirsha* (January-February) month amongst 12 months of the year; and in Spring, amongst seasons.

Of all skills in deceit, he is gambling; brilliancy of the brilliants; He is victory, the efforts and the goodness. He is Krishna Himself (Vasudeva), of the *Vrsnis* (clan of Yadavas); of the Pandavas, He is Arjuna, i.e., in Arjuna the Supreme is expressed most. Likewise, of sages, He is Vyasa, and of poets, He is Usana; of punishers, He is the Punishment; of seekers of victory, He is the wise policy; of secrets, He is the silence; of the achievers of wisdom, He is the Wisdom.

Concluding His Glory, Krishna says that He is the seed of all existence, and the principle to exist for all is He. The Divine manifestations of the Supreme are endless and infinite. Whatever is mentioned here are only a few examples of His Glory.

All the glorious, graceful and vigorous qualities in animates and inanimates have arisen from a minuscule aspect of His brilliance and splendour. To sum up, Krishna tells Arjuna that there is no need to go into such detail if one comprehends that the entire universe is supported and pervaded by the Supreme, by an iota of His Being, by a ray of His Light.

This is the essence of the tenth chapter of the *Gita*, entitled *The Yoga of Divine Glories*.

With our ordinary understanding, we cannot conceptualise the extent, potency, glory and greatness of the Supreme. This is because the mind is not a suitable instrument to measure the All-permeating, Omniscient God, as the mind works within the conditioned framework of Time-Space, and He is Timeless and Spaceless. It is, therefore, necessary to illustrate, with few examples, the splendour of God; such an exhibit of concept shall empower our mind in meditation upon Him.

Krishna has narrated arrays of such examples in the first person singular saying, e.g., "of the light, I am the Sun". This could be best understood if we realise that Krishna is the embodiment of the Supreme Self through whom the Truth was narrated. Krishna was One with Pure Consciousness by way of total merger in Him through Yoga.

There is no doubt that behind every phenomenon there is one single power functioning. This manifestation of the Supreme in 'living' and 'non-living' things could as well be seen in varying degrees of expression and multiple shades of illumination. For example, in human beings, it is more manifest than in animals or vegetation. Likewise, it is more visible in the mind and intellect than in gross sense organs.

Thus, by citing specific entities, Krishna demonstrates His relatively greater expression in virtues, talents, state of mind and happenings, the epicentres of powers and knowledge in various planes of time and experience and in celestial bodies. Ultimately, Krishna says that He Himself and Arjuna too are the focal points where the Supreme is more manifest than in others.

His virtues and glories are innumerable and if we take up one such quality for contemplation, the other godly qualities will automatically follow one by one. For example, if we take up fearlessness for empowerment in us, patience and calmness of mind shall follow. The characterisations of the Almighty are endless. The entire creation and existence/non-existence are supported and sustained by a ray of His Light, a streak of His Being. For the rest, we are not even capable of imagining It.

If during contemplation, and while living a worldly life, we think of this enormous phenomenon, we will be more compassionate, more kind-hearted, more hardworking, more loving, less fearful, less vengeful, less greedy, less unhappy and more spiritual. Wherever these qualities shine forth, we will bow in reverence remembering Him. Even in our own personality, in society, in Nature, or in our near-and-dear ones if we see godly traits, we should encourage these virtues, talents and capabilities for the betterment of the whole world.

Gita Gyana 10

- ❑ **10.1:** No one can know the origin of the Supreme because all originate from Him.
- ❑ **10.2:** He is Timeless and Spaceless – hence the mind and intellect cannot measure His extent because they function within the confines of time-space. But if the mind and intellect become silent and transcend time-space, He could be directly experienced.

- **10.3:** The sources of power and knowledge in the present as well as other planes of time-existence are verily illumined by His expression in varied shades.
- **10.4:** In the best amongst virtues, talents, experience, state of mind, happenings, prosperity, wisdom and love, He glitters most.
- **10.5:** His attributes are endless, His power is enormous and His totality is immeasurable.
- **10.6:** The Supreme is present in all, so discrimination on the basis of caste, creed, colour, wealth and power is wrong and baseless.
- **10.7:** Cultivate within yourself the knowledge of the truth, non-enchantment, self-control, calmness, fearlessness, non-violence, equipoise, contentment, austerity, love and compassion because they permeate via the Almighty to be expressed through you.
- **10.8:** Your fame, prosperity, good health, efforts, brilliance, victory, goodness and wisdom are a revelation of His glory and splendour. Foster them with care to flourish.
- **10.9:** Meditate on the multitude of attributes thus exemplified (a few) by Supreme Consciousness through Krishna – the Lord of Yoga.
- **11.0:** All is He and He is all; respect His brilliance strewn all over; love, don't hate; make efforts to ensure prosperity because He is both effort and prosperity!

10. Revere His Glory strewn all around you, then His glow of splendour will empower your life.

Chapter 11

The Infinite Cosmic Pattern

On listening to the preceding discourse, Arjuna tells Krishna that his bewilderment concerning the multi-dimensional manifestation of God has subsided, and he has learnt about the grandeur of Krishna. But he was still not content with the bright reflections of the Supreme as exemplified by Krishna; so, Arjuna wanted to 'see' the Divine Form of Krishna. To the human mind, the reality that is visible is more convincing than that which is heard only.

On hearing Arjuna's loving desire, Krishna graciously manifests His Divine Form, which Arjuna can directly 'behold' as a Divine Experience within his own Self. Krishna asks Arjuna to witness His Forms – hundred-folds, thousand-folds, of various shapes and colours. This stupendous multiplicity of creation is evident to us even in our worldly experience. Further, Arjuna is asked to view the custodians of powers at various planes of existence and time, the universe, and all that Arjuna desires to see! All in the Cosmic Form of Krishna!

But Krishna understands that Arjuna with his human physical eyes – with their limited power of sight – cannot catch even a glimpse of the Cosmic Manifestation; so He graced Arjuna with Cosmic Eyes – implying an intellectual power to perceive the direct knowledge of the Inconceivable. And, lo! Thereafter, Arjuna could envision the Cosmic Pattern with many mouths and eyes, many marvellous divine ornaments, numerous divine weapons in hands, wearing divine garlands, made up of all wonders, dazzlingly bright, boundless, facing all sides. However, this was just a prelude to the vastness and beatitude of the Cosmic Person.

The brightness of the Majestic Being could be compared with thousand suns shining at once in the sky. Wonderstruck – as he sees One in many and many in One – Arjuna tells Krishna: "In Your body, O God, I see all the gods and beings; *Brahma* and all the sages. I behold You, Infinite in form on all sides, with countless arms, abdomens, faces and eyes but I do not perceive your end, middle or beginning, O Lord of the universe!"

In awe, Arjuna continues to portray what he saw in the Cosmic Form of Krishna – crowns, mace, discus, glowing light, flaming fire, moons and suns, face in a glowing fire whose radiance burns up the universe; gods entering into the Eternal, all the possessor-beings of supernatural powers gazing at the Cosmic Form.

Arjuna watches the mouth of the Dynamic Figure open wide, with large glowing eyes. He trembles with fear and loses his bearings. He sees the Kauravas and their warriors, and also the fighters on his own side. All of them are rushing between the crushing jaws of the Cosmic Form. Arjuna, terrified, implores Krishna, praying and praising His Might; in horror, he requests Krishna to reveal who He is!

At this, the Blessed Lord says that He is Time, annihilating the world. Even if Arjuna does not fight and kill them, all the foes standing in opposing armies shall be killed. Therefore, clarifies Krishna, Arjuna must rise to the occasion, fight, conquer the kingdom and enjoy prosperity, as the foes have already been slain by Time. He wanted Arjuna to merely be a causal instrument in this process and to slay the mighty warriors, including elders, teachers, brethren and friends-turned-foes, standing in the opposite camp.

Arjuna witnesses the future; flabbergasted, he offers hymns of praise and devotion to Lord Krishna saying that

He is adored by gods and sages; He is the Infinite Being, Lord of the Universe, the Primal Person; Arjuna thus offers salutation to the Supreme Being and comprehends that the cosmic person in the embodiment of Krishna is Unlimited, Omniscient and All-pervading; he bows to Krishna in reverence, with folded hands and head inclined.

Krishna and Arjuna were bosom friends right from childhood. Now, at this moment of grand revelation, Arjuna reflects that during their long association he had committed several untoward acts against Krishna. Recognising Krishna's Cosmic Form, Arjuna feels guilty and seeks pardon for all that he might have done, not knowing the Almighty nature of Krishna. Arjuna prostrates before the Cosmic Form of Krishna, begs for His Grace and pardon and asks Him to tolerate him as a father does his son, as a friend does his friend and as a lover does his beloved.

Bewildered by the Unlimited Cosmic Dimensions of Krishna, Arjuna offers prayers with a request to Him to appear in the form of *Vishnu*, with four arms, of whom Krishna is an incarnation. On this, Krishna says that by His Grace and Divine Faculty, Arjuna was able to view the Cosmic Form – Universal, Primal, and Infinite, which no one else has seen and even gods are ever eager to see. That can neither be sighted by the study of *Vedas* nor by ritualistic sacrifices, charity, rituals or austerity. In the world of humans, no one can see His Cosmic Form that Arjuna has seen! Krishna tells Arjuna not to be afraid on seeing His All-pervasive Form. He tells him to behold again His previous form. Seeing the gracious human form of Krishna, Arjuna regains his composure.

Finally, Krishna asserts, "He who performs action for Me, he who makes Me the goal of his life, he who worships Me unattached and he who is free from enmity to all creatures, he goes to Me, O Pandava!"

This, briefly, is the essence of knowledge, devotional love, surrender and non-attached action – the complete Yoga.

This is the essence of the eleventh chapter of the *Gita*, entitled *The Yoga of the Vision of Cosmic Form.*

Arjuna had an intense desire to see the Cosmic Form of Krishna. But no one can 'see' or even comprehend the unlimited, all-pervasive phenomenon with limited and restricted sense organs. Hence, Krishna graces Arjuna with the Supreme Faculty to visualise the incomprehensible.

The Cosmic Form of Krishna as *Virat-Purusha* is a reality, not the imagination of a poet or daydreamer. Look around you – on earth, in water, in the sky, and consider your own self within, the functioning body, the mind, the intellect and the ego – and you may have a micro-glimpse of His Manifestation. Think of an atom, with electrons and neutrons revolving, energy particles emitting from the electron, dancing in space, splitting, fusing with each other, being annihilated and then again being created. Is this not a peep into the Cosmic Form?

The dance of life and death, passing through Time, is a perennial process. All have to perish: the oceans, the mountains, the organic and inorganic substances, even our sun! All are heading towards the crushing jaws of the Cosmic Form – Time – and the cycle of creation rotates endlessly. Who does not change? Only *Brahman*, the Absolute, the Self, the Cosmic Person, Consciousness, whom the rarest of rare may know!

The Cosmic Form can be thought of humbly if we ask: What are infinite gravity, infinite density, infinite speed in the black holes found in space? Where is the boundary of our universe? Even with the best devices and complex mathematical formulae, we cannot 'see' the boundary of our universe because it is expanding with the unimaginable speed of light – 300,000 kilometres per second! No device whatsoever can surpass this speed. Now do you get a glimpse of Cosmic Infinity?

So, believe in That Power. Behave according to the righteous rules laid down by the seers and sages of the past. Love the Supreme with devotion, worship, surrender, and try to 'behold' the Cosmic Experience all around you through silence and meditation.

The Spark is in all. Don't insult, hate, or have enmity with that Divine Spark. Perform actions in the glory of the Cosmic Person; try to attain Him by realising the energy within yourself; think of the power of the Infinite that creates, sustains and swallows one and all.

Gita Gyana 11

- ❑ **11.1:** Krishna reveals the Cosmic Form to Arjuna, comprehensible only by the Grace of the Almighty.
- ❑ **11.2:** All creation rushes towards death, and again, all is recreated through a cyclic system.
- ❑ **11.3:** Time is all-powerful; all exist in Time and all are annihilated through it.
- ❑ **11.4:** The Supreme is revered and worshipped by all Centres of Powers in the universe.
- ❑ **11.5:** In the Cosmic Pattern exist Brahmaji, all the godheads, worldly beings, sages, brightness of thousand suns and the totality of the glory.
- ❑ **11.6:** The exterior and the interior worlds in which we live – with all the wonders of life and Nature, thoughts and knowledge – are flashes of the Cosmic Form.
- ❑ **11.7:** Think beyond – and you cannot think; That is Limitless, Timeless, Spaceless, Deathless, Formless, with stupendous Beauty, Power, Glory, Serenity and Capabilities Unlimited.
- ❑ **11.8:** Even intellectual conceptualisation of the Cosmic Power may make us uneasy and restless; therefore, a more worldly form is to be meditated upon with which our mind is well acquainted. Or the formless Reality could be meditated upon.

- ❑ **11.9:** Reflections of the Cosmic Person are strewn all around us; so we must adore them by becoming loving, friendly, respectful, and compassionate towards all creatures and Nature.
- ❑ **12.0:** Lord Krishna reaffirms the significance of action: "Perform action for Me and make Me the goal of your life."

> **11. Look at the rising sun – you will see a ray of His Cosmic Form; look at a smiling baby – you will see a glow of His Cosmic Form; look at the flow of your thoughts – you will meet Dynamic Silence, which is the brilliance of His Cosmic Form.**

Chapter 12

Success Through the Yoga of Devotion

Arjuna asks Lord Krishna that from those who worship the Personal God manifested in the world and those who contemplate the Unmanifested *Brahman*, who has greater knowledge of Yoga?

Krishna answers that those who worship a Personal God in worldly form are perfect in Yoga. But those who worship the Unmanifested, Absolute *Brahman* by controlling their senses attain the goal of realisation, although it is more difficult for those attached to their bodies. Krishna says that those who remove their limitations by identifying themselves with the Form of their God by renouncing all actions in Him, meditate upon the Form of the Lord and make Him the goal of life are saved from conflicts of the world.

Krishna puts forth several alternative paths for spiritual uplift: If one focuses his mind and intellect on the God-Form he shall, no doubt, attain Him; if one is not capable of focusing his mind, he should practise concentration so that his inner self is gradually directed towards God; the third alternative, if the mind is unable to concentrate, is service of the Lord by performing actions for Him. Thus one achieves unfolding of the Self within. The fourth alternative is to take refuge in God, and act without attachment to the fruits of actions. This is the Yoga of desireless action.

Krishna indicates that knowledge (*gyana*) is better than the practice of concentration because it removes the darkness of ignorance and directs your spirit towards God. But meditation fills you with Him, i.e., God-Consciousness permeates your entire life; therefore, this is better than knowledge. Yet, even better than meditation is renunciation of the fruits of actions because it imparts peace and calmness of mind, which are the basics for divine revelation.

Now, Krishna enumerates the qualities of a true devotee, through which he receives the Grace of God and becomes dear to Him: One who has no ill will towards any being, who is friendly and compassionate, egoless, detached from happiness and unhappiness, and unperturbed.

Yogis who are ever content, self-controlled, firm in the path of devotion, and with mind and intellect surrendered to Him are dear to Him. Krishna mentions the righteous qualities through which the yogi interacts with the world outside: He who does not agitate the world around by his action and is also not agitated by chaotic conditions of the world, and he who is free from excessive joy and anger, and fear and restlessness, is dear to Him.

Krishna continues to enumerate the many virtues of a devotee: To whom criticism and praise is equal, who is silent (without superfluous chattering in the mind), content with anything, homeless (unattached to a place or dwelling), steady-minded and full of devotion – that man is dear to the Lord.

In the end, Krishna says that those who follow the immortal *dharma* with faith in the Supreme as the eternal aim of life are dearest to Him.

This is the essence of the twelfth chapter of the *Gita*, entitled *The Yoga of Devotion*.

There are two methods of attaining fulfilment through Yoga: one, contemplation upon the formless, abstract Absolute Reality – the Impersonal God, and two, worshipping the manifested Form of the Personal God. For meditation upon the Absolute, self-control and taming of the senses is a prerequisite; so also, joyfully working for the welfare of society, for the entire creation and Nature. Service in the name of the Almighty subdues the ego.

Krishna reveals several alternative approaches to uncover the inner self – concentration, knowledge (of the Self), meditation, and desireless action. No one method is better than the other *per se*. We must ascertain our capability to undertake the chosen method. There is no boundary separating one approach from the other; they silently merge into one another – if you start with one, it will lead to another even without your knowing it.

Ordinarily, for laypersons, knowledge, meditation, concentration, stilling the mind, etc, may be difficult. Therefore, it is suggested that the performance of action without desire for rewards is the best technique in Yoga for such individuals. But even surrendering the desire for rewards of action is difficult. Yet, if you stop worrying about the fruits of action, which dissipates your energy and pulls you forcibly into the future, you learn to be in the present moment and thus attain peace!

In the second part of this discourse, Krishna portrays the devotee who is dear to Him. Although all are dear to Him, the one who nurtures specific qualities gains His Grace faster. These include:

- **Lack of ill will towards any being:** This makes the mind serene and it does not gather any *vaasnas* (subtle tendencies).
- **Being friendly and compassionate:** This imparts purpose to our life.
- **Freedom from egotism and self-sense:** This relieves false pride.
- **Even-mindedness in pain and pleasure:** It frees one from conflicting dualities.
- **Patience:** Helps keep one's cool.

- **Ever content:** One does not abandon work but becomes detached from achievements.
- **Self-control:** Freedom from anger, greed, and wild desires accumulates no sin.
- **Firmness:** Keeps one steadfast, makes one actively determined and thus frees the person from grief.
- **Free from attachment:** No extreme attachment to anything, which could only bring sorrow.

The above are but a few qualities of an ideal devotee. Normally, we cannot observe many of them. But we can start with one or two traits and then notice the positive change in our life. The other virtues will then follow. When a devotee awakens into Pure Consciousness, dualities have no meaning for him. His aim is only the Supreme, and the Supreme definitely helps him.

Gita Gyana 12

- ❑ **12.1:** The Yoga of desireless action is best for worldly persons. It liberates one from the grip of anxiety about the future.
- ❑ **12.2:** Meditate regularly on the personal form of God. This ensures assimilation of Pure Consciousness into your being, leading to Bliss.
- ❑ **12.3:** Concentration on a form or the Formless Supreme dispels the wild dance of thoughts and expands your being.
- ❑ **12.4:** Knowledge about the changing pattern of creation against the backdrop of the Unchanging Supreme, and also about our Eternal *atman* and All-pervading *Brahman* must be sparked within.
- ❑ **12.5:** We must cultivate the qualities of a perfect devotee at all levels of personality.
- ❑ **12.6:** At the body level, observe cleanliness, abandon addictions, and be equipoised in heat and cold, pain and comfort and in other dualities.

- ❑ **12.7:** At the level of the mind, be friendly to all, compassionate, avoid desires and be alike in love, hate and other turbulent situations.
- ❑ **12.8:** At the intellectual level, work with skill and be self-controlled.
- ❑ **12.9:** At the ego level, be free of anger; don't react over-excitedly to honour or dishonour, praise and criticism etc.
- ❑ **13.0:** Let awareness in pure discernment (*chitta*) be devotion to the Creator, deep silence and total contentment; in the spirit, the awareness fixes the aim of achieving liberation.

12. Dissolve yourself in Him with love and devotion. He will absolve you.

Chapter 13

Fragrance of the Conscious Supreme

The illusion that wildly dances upon inert matter in the worldly system is removed by meditation, which unveils the spark of life that shines forth brilliantly. This is the ultimate aim of our life. To achieve this goal, a thorough knowledge of Nature (*Prakriti*, Field, Matter, *Kshetra*) and Spirit (*Purush*, Knower of the Field, *Atman*, *Kshetrajna*) is essential. Arjuna requests Lord Krishna to reveal the knowledge regarding the functioning of the Supreme (the Observer) through the media of worldly happenings.

Arjuna wanted to know about *Prakriti* and *Purusha*, the Field and the Knower of the Field, and Knowledge and the Object of the Knowledge. Krishna narrates that this body is called the Field and He who knows this is called the Knower of the Field. Thus, it implies that in the Field (body) all happenings take place and the Knower of the Field (Consciousness), inactive and detached, lies behind all activities. Krishna adds that He is the Knower of the Field. Describing various aspects of Field and the Knower of the Field, Krishna enumerates Five Great Elements (Space, Air, Fire, Water and Earth), egoism, intellectual tendencies, the five sense organs of perception and the five organs of action, the mind, the five objects of the senses (Taste, Touch, Sound, Sight, Smell), which in totality contribute to the constitution of the Field.

In addition to these, mental modifications of these attributes – desire, hatred, pleasure, pain, totality of the body, intelligence, calmness, etc – also make an integral part of the Field (*Prakriti*).

In brief, the entire knowable world is the Field (*Kshetra*; Object); the Knowing Essence is the Knower of the Field (*Kshetrajna*; Subject).

What is knowledge? The following qualities and their characteristics are enumerated by Lord Krishna, which become true Knowledge on adoption:

Humility, integrity, non-violence, patience, uprightness, reverence to the Guru, purity of body and mind, steadfastness of purpose, and self-control; non-attachment to sense objects, absence of egoism, thinking about evils in birth, death, old age, sickness and pain; non-passion, even-mindedness in loss or gain, undeviating Yoga of Devotion towards God, resort to solitary places or mental withdrawal into silence, distaste for crowds, consistency in knowledge of the Self, and sighting the ultimate end (aim, goal) towards True Knowledge.

All that is against this knowledge is ignorance. Further, Krishna describes THAT which is to be known, and by knowing which one achieves Life Eternal: It is the Supreme *Brahman*, Beginningless; neither Existent nor Non-existent – these states become superfluous from the viewpoint of the Transcendental State of the Supreme who is above and beyond every quality and phenomena. Pure Consciousness is All-pervading and All-enveloping.

In the marvellous functioning of all senses, His brilliance is visible, but He Himself does not possess any senses; He is unattached, yet He supports all; He is not defined by *gunas* (modes, qualities, attributes) yet He enjoys *gunas*. The Lord is outside as well as within all beings; moving as also unmoving; extremely subtle; far away and yet close. He cannot be divided and yet appears to be so amongst beings. He is to be known as the Sustainer, Destroyer and Creator as well.

He is the Knowledge, the Object of the Knowledge and the ultimate Aim of the Knowledge. To be worthy of His Estate, the devotee has to understand these facts so graciously revealed by Krishna.

Krishna now explains to Arjuna the concept of *Purusha* and *Prakriti.* He says that Matter (*Prakriti,* Nature) and the Spirit (*Purusha*) both are also beginningless, like the Supreme; varied modifications of forms are born from Matter (*Prakriti,* Nature). Thus Nature is the cause of the world of objects, and the Spirit (*Purusha*) is the cause of experience of pleasure and pain. The blissful nature of the Self, represented by the Spirit within the being, appears to be contaminated under the conditioned state and is stained by happiness and unhappiness because the Spirit identifies itself with the objects and becomes qualified by *Prakriti.* The Spirit seated in Nature enjoys the qualities born of Nature. Attachment to the qualities in Nature is the cause of its birth in good or evil wombs.

However, there is the Supreme Spirit (Supreme *Purusha*) also in the body, above and beyond, who is said to be a Silent Observer, the Permitter, the Supporter, the Experiencer, the Great Lord and the Supreme Self who illumines all the activities of *Prakriti* and *Purusha.* The person who thus knows the Spirit (*Purusha,* Soul) and Nature (*Prakriti,* Matter) together with their qualities attains freedom (liberation).

Krishna now reveals various paths leading to liberation. He says that some people follow Dhyana Yoga (meditation), others Gyana Yoga (the Yoga of Knowledge) and still others, Karma Yoga (the Yoga of Action). Yet others may simply worship on hearing about it from other persons; they, too, achieve Grace by their devotion.

The union of Nature and the Spirit manifests Creation. The Spirit lives equally in all beings but when the beings die, He still remains since He is imperishable. Injury to beings and to creation in any form is injury to one's True

Self. All actions are done by Nature while the True Self is only an Observer.

The various states of being are centred into One (the Immutable), from where they again radiate out. Thus, thought of limits and separatedness is degrading. The Supreme Self lives in the body but it neither acts nor gets tarnished by the results of actions because it has no qualities and no attributes. The Supreme is the Lord of the Field and illumines the whole Field just as one sun illumines the whole world.

By wisdom, the distinction between the Field (Nature, *Prakriti*, Matter, *Kshetra*) and the Knower-of the Field (Spirit, *Purusha*, Soul, *Kshetrajna*) should be perceived. So also one should understand the liberation of beings from Nature. A person who sees the truth and imbibes the knowledge described above attains the Supreme.

This is the essence of the thirteenth chapter of the *Gita*, entitled *The Yoga of Distinction Between the Field and the Knower of the Field.*

The Almighty, Eternal Lord is Beginningless, Immovable, the Silent Observer, One without a second, then how does the world of plurality agitated by pleasure and pain function? Unless we have knowledge of His nature – He acts and also acts not, etc – we cannot contemplate His Glory because the shadow of uncertain understanding will always haunt us. In order to perceive the knowledge (of the True Self), we must learn to live with high moral values imbibed in the body-mind-intellect-ego system of our personality.

The characteristics of Reality cannot be described because all the instruments for description (mind, intellect, vocabulary, etc) are limited in their capabilities while He is Unlimited. Sages of the *Upanishads* have rightly declared God as "*Neti-Neti.*" That is, He is this, yet He is not this. To us unenlightened beings, this may sound confusing and contradictory. Yet it is said that He is neither existent nor non-existent; He is neither active nor inactive, and so on. With reference to the Supernatural State and Transcendental Reality, existence and activity or other qualities that attempt to delimit Reality become meaningless, illogical and superfluous.

Suppose we ask a person to describe 'space' (*Aakash*, Ether), what will he reply? It will be some unspecific, arbitrary description! Space is an experience rather than an entity. Similarly, God is an inner experience rather than a descriptive unit.

God is everywhere, Omnipresent, like the 'particles' in modern particle Physics. The field of energy connects the whole universe known so far to us. The universe is full of atoms and their constituents – electrons, protons, neutrons and several types of their components (particles). All are dancing in the so-called 'void' but actually there is no void. All space is filled with energy and matter (sub-nuclear). This energy is indestructible and it plays through matter. If you reduce energy, matter increases, and vice versa. This comparison may give some glimpse of *purusha* (energy) and *prakriti* (matter) although the simile is not complete because the God factor is much beyond it.

The world of objects is born of Nature (*prakriti*) and the experience of pleasure and pain are occurrences in the Spirit. Although a God factor itself, under certain situations the Spirit gets attached to experiences of pleasure and pain. Once the Spirit is free and recognises itself, it again becomes one with the Supreme.

This freedom of the Spirit is liberation (*moksha*, salvation). That is our aim. To achieve this, we do not have to wander outside in the world. Practise the path shown by those who have been graced by the experience of Reality and search within. He lives there!

Any hurt, injury or injustice done by you against any creature or towards Nature, in any way, shall increase your bad *karma* because He is present in all. Understand that the real fulfilment and happiness, the bliss, lies within you and can be evoked when He is served through His creation. Help the poor, the destitute, the have-nots, life in general and Nature. Then see the magic!

Liberate yourself from the illusion of *prakriti* while living and acting within it. You are Pure Consciousness but at present your Spirit has become ignorant of its real nature in the company of *maya* (illusion) of *prakriti* (Nature). Therefore, the Spirit is acting as ego (*jiva*) with its limitations.

Remove the veil of darkness and let the Sun of knowledge shine.

Gita Gyana 13

- ❑ **13.1:** *Prakriti* is constituted by five gross elements plus the totality of our body, our mental construct, the sense organs and their objects. *Prakriti* is unaware but active.
- ❑ **13.2:** The Knowing Principle is the Spirit (*Purusha*), which is a reflection of the Eternal Supreme. The *Purusha* is not involved in action Himself but is aware about all.
- ❑ **13.3:** While expressing itself through Nature, the Spirit gets partially conditioned by the qualities of Nature and forgets its own blissful singularity while functioning inside Nature.
- ❑ **13.4:** The veiled Spirit (soul), thus functioning inside inert Nature, behaves as the *jiva* and suffers the pleasure and pain of its deeds. Worldly pleasure is also a suffering because it is doomed to be lost shortly.
- ❑ **13.5:** When the veil of ignorance is lifted by the practice of positive qualities and values, the Spirit again emits light and the dualities of Nature vanish.

These virtues become knowledge in themselves when imbibed.

- ❑ **13.6:** Knowledge of the God-Principle – Beginning-less, Eternal, Limitless, Creator, Sustainer and Annihilator of all, neither existent nor non-existent, neither performer nor non-performer, is essential for contemplation.
- ❑ **13.7:** The God-Principle is present in every creature, in Nature and in all creation. Hence, we must not hurt any beings or the environment.
- ❑ **13.8:** The Supreme is expressed through Nature (including our body) but He is not involved. He acts as the bright light of the Sun, illumining all good or bad, as an Observer.
- ❑ **13.9:** Perform hard work but do not get entangled in the reward (Karma Yoga). With the support of the knowledge of Truth, devotion, and the practice of established values of *dharma*, you are sure to attain Freedom.
- ❑ **14.0:** Freedom (salvation, liberation, *moksha*) is our goal. Permanent happiness (bliss) can come only through this path, along with meditation upon Him. The world is the play of the Supreme. The moment you get established in this state of wisdom, the world of pleasure and pain dissolves. This is salvation!

13. The Sun dances in the lake, the Spirit dances in Nature, but both are like the superimposition of a snake on the rope.

Chapter 14

Inborn Attitudes: Gears of Progress

Lord Krishna again explains to Arjuna about the Supreme Wisdom by knowing which seers achieved perfection. Krishna says that by gaining this wisdom, one becomes like Him (the Supreme) in nature and transcends the mind to realise the Eternal Self within; thereafter, he neither experiences the agony of birth at the time of Creation nor of death at the time of Dissolution. Krishna tells Arjuna that He casts the seed in *prakriti*, the womb of the Supreme (i.e. the primordial aspect of Creation) and then all beings are born. Thus, *prakriti* is the mother and God is the father of all beings. And since *prakriti* is the Nature of God, He is the mother as well as father of all Creation.

Now, Lord Krishna describes *gunas* (modes, inherent attitudes of being, influence originating from core thoughts and behaviours, immanent nature of being, etc). There are three types of *gunas*:

- *Sattva*: Purity, goodness, illumination
- *Rajas*: Passion, compulsive movement for action
- *Tamas*: Dullness, inertia, negligence, indifference, darkness

The *gunas* are born of *prakriti* (Nature) but bind the indestructible Dweller (Soul) of the body. Thus, when the Soul identifies itself with the *gunas* of Nature, it forgets its Eternal Essence and gets entangled in the world through the body-mind-intellect-ego (which are the attributes of inert

Nature). These *gunas* are, thus, bondages; therefore, one must try to rise above all three to attain liberation.

Describing the characteristic of each *guna*, Lord Krishna says that *sattva* generates the light of knowledge (Truth) and a sense of well-being but still produces bondage to 'happiness' and to intellectual glamour (through the remnant of ego). It implies that even goodness makes you limited if your ego plays through it.

Rajas (passion) plays on attraction and is generated from attachment to action with desire and anxiety. *Rajas* binds beings to *prakriti* by enchantment to compulsive activity.

Tamas (inertia) is the product of ignorance. It generates bondage through negligence, laziness, sleep, and not paying heed to self-evolution.

At a given time, all three *gunas* are present and function in a being but one of the three predominates while the other two may be subdued.

What are the symptoms when one or the other *guna* (attitude) is dominant in a person? Krishna explains that when *sattva* (purity) increases, the light of knowledge shines into the mind and all the senses become 'aware' about the true nature of the object, the world and Divine Reality. When *rajas* increases, greed, activity (with attachment), beginning of undertaking (with the ego sense of a doer), agitation (due to non-fulfilment), and desires (unwarranted, unnatural, unnecessary wishes) come to the fore. When *tamas* increases, dimness (of the light of knowledge), inactivity, negligence and deception arise in the being.

If at the time of departure of the Soul, *sattva* (goodness) is in dominance, the being attains a plane of existence that wise sages attain. Further, if death occurs when *rajas* is prominent, one is born amongst those who are attached to action. And dying in the dominance of *tamas*, one is born in the womb of the dull (deluded, sluggish, senseless, foolish).

The fruit of *sattva* is purity; the fruit of *rajas* is pain, and the fruit of *tamas* is ignorance. From goodness and purity arises knowledge (of the Divine); from passion arises greed; and from dullness arises faults and ignorance. Those established in *sattva* evolve upwards; the *rajasic* remain in the middle (of the ladder of spiritual progression); and the *tamasic* are involved completely in the function of the lowest attitude of life.

When the seer beholds no other agent (media) than the *gunas* (which work through his being) and transcends his own mind beyond the *gunas*, he attains the Supreme, i.e., his Soul is liberated from all the *gunas* and remains no more a hostage of any circumstance – good or evil. His Soul thus attains its original Eternal Abode.

To become free, even *sattvic* goodness is to be crossed over because it also gets attached with goodness and happiness. Goodness and purity also hanker for their own protection. One must remove the thorn in the flesh of one's foot by the help of another bigger thorn -- then throw away both thorns!

On hearing this, Arjuna asks Lord Krishna how to recognise the one who has risen above the three *gunas*? How does one achieve this state of Supra-*gunas* and leap beyond the three *gunas*?

Krishna answers that a person who neither fancies nor hates illumination, activity and delusions; unconcerned (towards *gunas*); regards pain and pleasure alike; dwells in the Self (contemplating); looks upon a piece of clay, stone or gold alike; unshakable in pleasant and unpleasant situations; who is firm; who regards honour and dishonour equally; is the same with friends and foes, and who has given up all initiatives (with the sense of ego as a beginner), he is said to have elevated himself above the *gunas*. He who surrenders unto the Supreme with unfailing devotion of love (*bhakti*) rises above the three *gunas*. Krishna says that He is the Abode of *Brahman* – meaning that the Immortal, Imperishable Pure Consciousness fully glows in Lord Krishna. He is also the Abode of *dharma* and Absolute Bliss.

This is the essence of the fourteenth chapter of the *Gita*, entitled *The Yoga of Gunas.*

Nature is the Mother and the Supreme is the Father of all creatures. Since Nature is the manifestation of the Supreme Himself, the Supreme is the Mother as well as Father of all. For selfish desires, man exploits Nature, disturbs the environment and pollutes the air, water, and land; consequently, he shall suffer from cumulative sins. Hence, do not hurt Mother Nature. Rather, support its loving expression that is God Himself.

Every person acts in this world under the influence of his personality, thoughts and intelligence. These attributes are known as *gunas*. They could be visible as purity, passion or inertia in each person. By following certain paths of right living, one can slowly change his traits from inertia to passion and from passion to purity; the last one is the path of freedom; ultimately *sattva* (purity) is also to be overcome fully so that no *guna* remains to be hankered after.

One must analyse himself and his own state of the dominating *guna*. Dullness, lethargy, inattentiveness, negligence, inactivity, ignorance about Divine Knowledge, and confused perception of the world, etc, comprise *tamas*. By practice and firm determination, these states can be altered to alertness, awareness, activeness, peace and tranquillity, while performing dynamic actions.

Similarly greed, craving, wild desires, hyper-activity to accumulate excessive luxury and wealth by fair or foul means, agitated, turbulent mind, unstable thoughts, etc, constitute *rajas*. The practice of detachment from the anxiety of rewards, thus taming anxiety about the future, and by becoming compassionate, helping the have-nots, nature and humanity, shall turn passion into positive activity with peace of mind, and *sattva* will arise in due course of time. While *rajas* is not bad *per se*, one must be aware of the turmoil and unhappiness it generates because of pain-creating attachment with greed and never-ending wild desires.

Sattva (purity) expresses itself through calmness of mind, purity of thoughts, devotion to God and equipoise in all circumstances. This is the highest of all states and it must be finally transmuted into the illumination of knowledge and the serenity of Bliss.

In the present world, with the disarray of modern times, inertia leads to self-destruction. Work you must, and with full zeal and vigour. *Rajas* in the present competitive times may be fine but the stress, family discord, the hazard of children going astray, ultimate breakdown of health, lack of tranquillity, and a feeling of emptiness while departing are definitive outcomes of such passion and greed. So watch out for these hazards.

The *Gita* is very assertive about all that is told here. These analyses of human personality, of their relational affinities and pleasure and pain, are based upon direct experiences of sages during enlightenment through deep meditation.

The essence of this discourse is to act to achieve with a detached attitude; abandonment of greed, hate, dualities of pain and pleasures; to be firm and determined; not to be perturbed by honour or dishonour, but to act. Devotion to the Lord with love and a sense of service is the key to freedom from grief, and the way to real happiness.

Gita Gyana 14

- ❑ **14.1:** God is the mother and father of all Creation.
- ❑ **14.2:** The spark of life within, as the Soul, is the expression of God Himself glowing through our body.
- ❑ **14.3:** In this system, the soul is partially veiled by the qualities of *prakriti* and thus forgets its real nature.
- ❑ **14.4:** Purity, passion, and inertia are three attitudes that function through us in various modes of predominance.
- ❑ **14.5:** These are three *gunas* that create attachment, resulting in pain.

- **14.6:** Get above all the three by generating calmness of mind, detachment from anxiety about the fruits of action and attracting serene illumination of Divine Knowledge.
- **14.7:** Overcome *tamas* by destroying negligence, laziness, ignorance, lethargy, dullness, etc. Overcome *rajas* by righteous activity, a balanced life in all aspects subduing greed as well as such work that does not give a sense of fulfilment.
- **14.8:** After being established in *sattva* by good work, try to absorb these traits, and keep away from ego-sense of happiness, knowledge and purity thus obtained.
- **14.9:** The Eternal Natural Law of life (*dharma*) is our aim for practice.
- **15.0:** All-pervading Consciousness functions through all beings and also through Nature by way of *gunas*. Meditate upon this wisdom and attain freedom!

> **14. Unattached action is *sattvic.* Attached action is *rajasic.* No action is *tamasic.* So, act you must but counteract you must not!**

Chapter 15

Freedom and Bliss

To continue the unfolding of the deeper knowledge about the Supreme and *prakriti*, Krishna says that having its roots above and branches below, the imperishable *Asvattham* (*Peepal* tree) represents the Tree of Life. Its leaves are *Vedas* (knowledge of the Supreme Self), and one who achieves this knowledge attains Totality of Knowledge – the Truth. The Tree represents the Cosmic Manifestation; it draws its energy from the Supreme through its roots being upwards. The branches are widespread, showing activities of various sorts, nourished by the *gunas;* the twigs are sense objects. This is the process of the cosmos.

The jumbling of the branches and twigs of this tree of the world, limitless in extension, has to be cut through by the strong sword of non-attachment, and thus a path of self-evolution is to be made! It implies that the worldly chaos of sense objects and pleasure and pain could be crossed over only by getting rid of the entanglement and bondage in the web of the tree of life. In order to realise Pure Consciousness high up there (conceptual level of greatness) from which this tree gets its nourishment for the worldly system below, one must understand this cosmic tree.

To reach that Eternal State, one has to follow the path of those who have already attained That and completely surrender with love and devotion to the Eternal Supreme. Also, by abandoning pride, delusion, attachment, desires and dualities, one may achieve the goal of perfection.

Krishna continues that the life in the world, as expressed by the Supreme, is only a ray of His Self. The sun, the moon, or fire cannot illumine His place. Those who attain His place don't return in the cycle of life and death. When the Light of Consciousness illumines all the sources of light, the sun, the moon, fire, etc, how can they illumine Consciousness Itself?

Krishna says that a ray of His aspect (or an Expression of His Grandeur) becomes a soul and pulsates as life in the world. When the soul comes in contact with *prakriti* (Nature), it functions through the five senses (*gyanendryas,* senses of perception) and the mind. In other words, the senses and their allied qualities function only when the Spirit illumines them, although the Spirit is not involved in the function. But when conditioned by the mind and the intellect of a person, the iota of the aspect of the Supreme (the soul) appears to behave as *jiva* (ego) and takes various embodiments. When a person dies, the soul 'leaves' the body, attracts the senses as well as the mind (including intellect and emotions) and takes them to another body, as the breeze takes the fragrance from its source, say flowers. It means that the subtle body moves along with the soul in its journey to another plane of existence.

The *jiva* dwelling in *prakriti,* and thus conditioned, enjoys objects of the senses, through the ears, eyes, skin, tongue, nose, and also the mind. Actually the Eternal, although expressed through *jiva,* neither acts nor enjoys objects but is reflected in the *jiva* as if He, the Eternal, enjoys.

Krishna explains the complex illusion of the soul-body-world system by saying that even when He (the soul, the ray of the Eternal) departs from the body, or lives in the body or experiences worldly objects in association with the *gunas,* ignorant persons do not recognise the presence of the Eternal Being. But the wise "see" Him. Even those who strive but are indisciplined and unintelligent cannot find Him. The question arises: Where does one "see" Him?

Lord Krishna points out that the glory of the light in the sun, the moon and the fire shines forth from His

Grandeur. All beings are supported by His vital energy passing through the earth; the essence in all the vegetation is nourished by the life principle, which is none other than He. The Eternal Soul is the warmth and the energy of life in the beings that, in association with life-sustaining breath, carries out all functions in various systems of the body.

The Eternal One lives in the heart (bosom) of all beings. The faculty of memory and knowledge and so also that of the withdrawal of remembrance from undesirables operate because of Him. The Lord is the ultimate goal to reach by the practice of worship and prayers cited in the *Vedas*; He is the compiler of *Vedanta* – the synthesis and unified knowledge of all the *Vedas* in which only One Supreme is projected. And in reality, only a perfectly pure-hearted being may identify himself with Pure Consciousness and only he (one who is established in the Self) can know the Supreme Knowledge (the *Vedas*).

Further, illuminating the aspect of the Supreme Person, Krishna says that there are two *Purushas* in the world – the Perishable and the Imperishable. One who is changeable is perishable (the realm of existences) and the other, the unchangeable, is known as the Imperishable (Spirit, Conscious Principle). But the highest is other than these two, known as the Highest Spirit – the Supreme Self, the Indestructible Lord who sustains and supports the whole creation. Thus, mutable is the changing universe, and the Immutable is the power of the Lord (the soul), and the Supreme which is said to be Eternal, Pure and Intelligent, and free from limitations of mutable as well as immutable.

Krishna concludes that for the wise being who knows Him as the Supreme *Purusha,* nothing remains to be known. Such an enlightened one worships Him with his sublime inner being. By knowing this, by realising the highest state of *Purushottama* (the Supreme *Purusha*) a person will become wise and by being established in the state of the Highest, one will attain Bliss.

This is the essence of the fifteenth chapter of the *Gita*, entitled *The Yoga of the Supreme Person.*

The cosmic system is beyond the comprehension of our ordinary sense organs and the mind. However, it must be understood that the world gets its life energy from the Supreme and a path to perceive Him could be made by cleaning the clutter of entanglement in our lives. While living and acting in the world, we have to withdraw our clinging and attachment from the objects of senses that bind us.

Egotistic pride and the sense of false self-esteem lead to pain. Uncontrolled longings and agitating dualities in day-to-day living create turmoil in our heart. Then where are peace and perfection? Intensive awareness about the functioning of the entire complex system of our outer and inner dimensions is needed to know ourselves with reference to the universe.

A spark of the Supreme makes our body function. That Eternal Power cannot be 'seen' directly but can definitely be experienced within by way of surrender to its source. The energy, in whatever form, is indestructible. Thus, it could be understood that after the death, the Eternal Spark 'moves' out of the body and takes along with it our accumulated *karma* – good or evil, our tendencies and unfulfilled desires – to the other plane of existence. The energy thus transferred to the other womb manifests there for further expression because it is not destroyed; hence it must be transmuted. A ray of the tiny aspect of the Supreme is the courier of the totality of our *karma*, including our *gunas* (attitudes). *Vaasna* in the subtlest form is the material and our *jiva* (ego) is the enjoyer or sufferer!

Although the Supreme appears to be playing in the perishable elemental world (as Nature, and its qualities: body, mind and their attributes), and also as the life-factor (the Eternal Spark, the Spirit, the Imperishable), the Highest Self is above and beyond these two integrals of the *Lila* or

Cosmic Play. The Highest Self, Pure Consciousness is beyond all descriptions and imagination of our limited and conditioned mind as well as intelligence. Under His Illumination, all happens – but He remains a Dynamic Silence!

If we are ourselves indisciplined and unaware intellectually, we will never be able to recognise the qualities and talents of others. Then however hard you try, no harmony, peace or success can be achieved in the family, in society, at your workplace or extensively in human systems unless every individual lives a disciplined life with a livewire intelligence of alertness.

Our health is a boon of the Supreme, disseminating for us from the water, air, earth, vegetation, sun, moon and other phenomena in Nature. Therefore, we must maintain our body to remain fit and also support the vital factors around us to let them remain viable; they are His instruments for our happiness.

Various concepts about God, godheads, symbols and entities, living or nonliving, with form or formless, are a pointer towards ONE SUPREME and all prayers, rituals, actions of devotion and philosophies are aimed at ONE SUPREME. Then why are there discrepancies and violence in the name of faith, religion, cult or concept? Fighting for the supremacy of our own faith is a crime against the Supreme.

Our body, and all that is related to it, is changing every moment; our Spirit is non-changeable. But the Supreme Highest is beyond change and non-change. He cannot be conditioned by any adjective. He simply Is.

Therefore, to achieve blissful happiness and a serene sense of fulfilment, one must establish oneself in the highest state of Pure Consciousness. The technique of achieving such an aim in life is taught herein.

Gita Gyana 15

- 15.1: There is only one source of Eternal Energy.
- 15.2: There is only one source of Eternal Intelligence.
- 15.3: That source can be experienced within ourselves by cleaning our bosom from clutter.
- 15.4: Ego-coated pride is painful in the end.
- 15.5: Wild desires, uncontrolled longings and reaction towards pairs of opposites create turmoil in the mind.
- 15.6: Perfection can be accomplished by abandoning delusion and bondage of passion.
- 15.7: Life in the world is a ray of His Glow, His Expression – contemplate on the Whole.
- 15.8: Our *karma* – including the essence of our acts, ego, intellect, mind and desires – move after death along with *jiva,* in the form of subtlest energy and get implanted in the other womb suitable for expression; this cycle of indestructible energy goes on, only transmutating from one form to another.
- 15.9: It is wise to recognise His manifestations in this world.
- 16.0: By knowing the Cosmic System, choosing one's individual path, learning the ideals of those who have attained the Truth, and by establishing oneself in the higher state of Divine Knowledge, nothing remains to be known.

15. The world is only a ray of the Supreme Glow. Can you think of the Totality?

Chapter 16

Let Divine Light Radiate!

Krishna narrates characteristics of divine-natured and demon-natured minds amongst beings of the world. He enumerates that:

- Fearlessness, purity of heart, steadfastness in the Yoga of Knowledge, charity, control of senses, sacrifice (surrender to Him), study of scriptures, austerity and integrity;
- Non-violence, truth, absence of anger, renunciation, calmness, absence of crookedness, compassion for living beings, absence of senseless hunger for possession, gentleness, modesty, and absence of fickleness of mind;
- Vigour, forgiveness, strength of mind, purity, absence of hatred, absence of pride....

...are qualities of a person born in divine nature. Such positive attributes to attain perfection and peace in life can also be adopted as guiding factors by those who desire to walk on the divine path.

Now, contrasting the above virtues of divinely structured qualities in man, Krishna enumerates the virtue-less, disgraceful, darker characteristics of the demonic type due to which one is involved in excessive pride and sensual gratification. He says that hypocrisy and erroneous self-glorification, anger, harsh behaviour and ignorance (about the Self) are characteristics of the one who is born of a demonic nature.

Krishna continues to elaborate the consequence of such divine and demonic attributes by saying that divine characters are destined for freedom (of the Self from pain and pleasure) and the demonic are doomed to slavery (bondage). He assures Arjuna that he was born with divine qualities and hence should not grieve.

Again, elaborating the characteristics of the demonic, Krishna says that a demonic person is ignorant about righteous action or renunciation; he is devoid of purity, good conduct and the truth. Such ignorant, cruel beings do not accept the existence of the Supreme Reality, of All-sustaining Truth, and of the God that is the cause of all. Engaged in wicked deeds, they are enemies of the world. Their desires can never be satisfied; they are full of double-speak, extremely proud of themselves and arrogant; they are confused in views and act upon impure decisions.

Obsessed with disheartened apprehension and anxiety for their selfish objectives, they meet death engaged in lustful desires, thinking it to be the ultimate aim of life. They perspire to amass fabulous wealth and superfluous luxury by evil and corrupt means, just to satisfy their longings. Such people arrogantly say: "This is achieved by me; this desire I shall fulfil; this wealth is mine. No one is as great as I am." Obviously, such people deceive themselves with ignorance. Bewildered and confused by wild thoughts, addicted to lust and entangled in cobwebs of delusion, they fall into hell – a mental state of torture, pain, agony and unhappiness – because of misleading judgements about the world.

Such people are born again and again in the womb of demons only, and if they remain deluded (in falsehood) birth after birth, not trying to attain divine qualities, they go further down in degradation into the sorrowful plane of existence.

Krishna indicates that man should abandon lust, anger and greed because they push him into hell – a state of mental turmoil, unhappiness, pain and imperfection. One who has crossed these three gates of darkness, and he who practises what is good for him, achieves liberation. Not following the light of scriptures and acting under the impulse of his own desire, one cannot attain perfection, happiness or the Supreme Goal.

The final directive of Krishna is that the scripture should be taken as an authority in determining what should be done and what should not be done. After knowing these rules and following the ordinance of the scripture, one must do his work.

This is the essence of the sixteenth chapter of the *Gita*, entitled *The Yoga of Distinction Between Divine and Demonic Inherence.*

The overall tendencies and attitudes in human beings can be classified into two types of realms: one, value-based qualities that are humane, positive, stable peace and happiness, spiritual and divine; two, valueless qualities that are non-humane, negative, a source of agitation and unhappiness to the self as well as to others, spiritually devolutionary and demoniacal. Each one of these traits is related either with the mind (through intelligence, ego, emotions) or to speech (behaviour, expression, pronouncements), or even to your work (act, performance, planning, system, etc).

No single person may possess either positive or negative characteristics exclusively; they are mixed in varying degrees and also vary at different periods in life. But our aim should be to strive for cultivating divine qualities and abandoning demonic ones.

Interestingly, all these intrinsic features, positive or negative, are linked like a chain, and if somebody masters one of the positive qualities, the other divine character will follow, destroying the negative counterpart of the same. Such change occurs so smoothly that not much effort is needed to keep the chain reaction going, once the first step is taken.

We spend our precious life in senseless pursuit of material things, as well as vanity. These superfluous materials and futile activities are of no consequence, and become painful within a short time. We are disillusioned and desperate when there is loss of possession. So where is happiness? It is in the knowledge of the Reality and Truth.

Dominated by arrogance, lust and pride, the demoniacal mind starts hating others – including the spouse, children, friends, humanity, God and ultimately the Self. This is hell!

Here, Lord Krishna gives a formula. Lust, anger and greed are to be abandoned first, one by one, and then see the magic of His Grace! Finally, when you are in doubt about the ethics of something and unable to decide the righteous path of action, virtues or even definitions of values, consult the scripture, interpret it positively in the context of changing times, strike a balance, and then act. Grace will be yours!

Gita Gyana 16

- ❑ **16.1:** Human nature can be classified as: (a) divine (b) diabolical (extremely wicked and cruel).
- ❑ **16.2:** Divine traits are value-based, life supportive, peace-generating, God-oriented and humane.
- ❑ **16.3:** Demoniacal qualities are inhumane, negative, pain-creating, anti-world and anti-divine.
- ❑ **16.4:** No one possesses exclusively positive or negative traits; the path is shown here to strive and achieve the positive.
- ❑ **16.5:** The negative path will neither lead to materialistic gains nor spiritual enlightenment.
- ❑ **16.6:** Insatiable wild desires, terrifying insecurity and deluded view of life are the result of a demonic state.
- ❑ **16.7:** Quietude of mind, stable happiness through compassion and tolerance, the Yoga of Knowledge and discovery of the Self are the natural outcome of divine traits.

- ❑ **16.8:** Balanced life is achieved through hard work, rational attunement with the world outside and inside, consistency in purpose, integrity of character and curbing of torturous desires.
- ❑ **16.9:** Lust, anger and greed eventually annihilate your happiness and peace of mind.
- ❑ **17.0:** When in doubt about your duty, ethics and lifestyle, follow the sayings of the scripture, adopt them to the system of living and act. Don't leave the basics of the *Gita*. Strike a balance in life by attuning and readjusting relational systems to the positive.

16. Follow one virtuous trait honestly; the next will follow you earnestly.

Chapter 17

Evolve by Efforts and be Free

It has been ascertained that in case of doubt, a man must follow the guidelines laid down in the scripture. However, Arjuna's inquisitive mind prompts him to request Lord Krishna to elaborate upon the situation where one does not understand or know the rules but still worships with love and devotional faith. He wants to know whether such an act falls under the nature of good (*sattva*), passionate (*rajas*), or dull (*tamas*) *gunas* (attitudes)! On hearing this, Lord Krishna vividly describes the relational affinities of the three *gunas* with respect to faith, kind of food, sacrifices (service to others), austerity (*tapas*, penance, voluntary self-denial), charity (alms-giving, donation – *daan*), renunciation and relinquishment.

Krishna says that according to the innate attitude of one's nature (*gunas*), faith (*shradhdha*, noble devotional essence of the entire being; love; respect; reverence) is categorised as *sattvic* (balanced joy), *rajasic* (passionate; active) and *tamasic* (careless, dull). The man is characterised by the faith he keeps. The good, serene man with virtuous traits (*sattvic*) worships God, Supreme Consciousness; the *rajasic* (active, agitating, eager for power and wealth) invokes deities of wealth (*Yakshas*) and strength (*Asuras*); and the *tamasic* (dull, ignorant) worships lowly, unscrupulous evil spirits, ghosts and the elements of darkness. Propelled by the force of lust and passion, these people perform troublesome austerities (self-agonising practice, dark *tapas*) that are demonic.

Good people (*sattvic*) have a liking for food that promotes life, vitality, strength, health, joy and cheerfulness and that are sweet, soft, nourishing and agreeable; while the *rajasic* like bitter, sour, salty, very hot, pungent, dry and burning food that creates pain and disease; and the *tamasic* like stale, tasteless, rotten leftovers and impure food.

Krishna now deals with the act of sacrifice. In the *Gita*, sacrifice (*yagna*) has a different connotation, unlike that of *Vedic* times, as it refers to selfless service of humanity, even to the extent of self-pain and discomfort. Krishna says that such *yagna* is of three kinds: *sattvic* is as per the scripture, without any expectations of reward or for show, but as a duty. But if one offers service with expectations of a reward, or for show, it is *rajasic*. In the *tamasic* sacrifice, no rule is followed, no charity is given, no praise of God is chanted, and even food is not distributed to the poor.

In the practice of Yoga and for the attainment of Eternal Knowledge, purity of mind is a prerequisite. Therefore, *tapas* (austerity, self-control) is given the utmost significance, in order to remove impurities. Krishna says that the worship of Gods, of the realised ones, of teachers and wise men, besides practising righteousness, self-control and non-violence, constitutes *tapas* of the body. Inoffensive talks that are truthful, pleasant and beneficial to all, and regular recitation of the *Vedas* is the *tapas* of speech. The *tapas* of mind comprise calmness, gentleness, silence (including that of thought), self-control and purity of thoughts.

Talking about *daan* (donation), Krishna says that *daan* given as duty, at a proper time and place to a worthy person, without any expectations of return is *sattvic*. But charity made in the hope of reward, or when it is unpleasant to give, is *rajasic*. Further, *daan* made at the wrong place, wrong time, to an unworthy person, or without due respect is *tamasic*.

For perfecting the act of sacrifice, giving gifts, austerity, etc, Krishna shows the right way by saying: "*Aum Tat Sat*", which is the threefold symbol of *Brahman*. From this, the *Brahmins* (the knower of *Brahman*), the *Vedas* and sacrifices (*yagna; tapas*) originated. *Aum* expresses the Absolute, the Infinite Substratum; *Tat* the universality, and *Sat* the existence. To invoke the Supreme, this mantra is chanted for each action to purify its purpose. Before the act of sacrifice, gift and *tapas, Aum* is uttered. While performing these acts, *Tat* is uttered. *Sat* also means praiseworthy action surrendered to Existence. Steadfastness in sacrifice, *tapas* and the gift is also called *Sat*.

In the end, Krishna cautions that whatever offering or gift is made, whatever *tapas* is performed and whatever sacrifice is done, without faith it is *asat* – of no consequence here or hereafter.

This is the summary of the seventeenth chapter of the *Gita,* entitled *The Yoga of Threefold Division of Faith.*

If any person does not know or understand the laws laid down in the scripture, what should he do? Answers to these questions are meticulously given. All the acts of virtuous nature are related to threefold influences or *gunas:* good (*sattvic*), passionate (*rajasic*) and dull (*tamasic*). The acts of faith, our diet, the help we extend to others, the self-denial or self-control we observe for our purification, the charity we offer, the non-attachment we practise, each of these acts is categorised as high, medium and low depending on our attitude.

Worshipping with faith in One Eternal Supreme liberates us; selfless service of humanity makes us happy; charity to the right person for the right cause is satisfying; keeping healthy by right eating is joyous; austerity of high quality at body, mind and speech level is a purifier of our self. Performing all acts of goodness in the name of the Absolute, Universal Existence (Pure Consciousness) creates quietude in life and disciplines our ego.

In none of these ethical and virtuous practices should there be an iota of desire for rewards, repayment, vanity, fame, or show. If at heart, the purpose of performance is pure, the Grace of Pure Consciousness is assured. But without faith and firm belief (*shradhdha*) even good work is futile. Faith in God, humanity, and virtuous deeds and in ourselves shall liberate us.

Aum Tat Sat is the cosmos and even beyond! No one can describe It because our mind is limited and the Absolute is Unlimited. We can only imbibe It in our self through symbols and concepts, and experience That in contemplation. Meditation opens the gate towards transcendental Reality that no words can delimit. We have to strive hard for attaining the *sattvic* way of life. Ultimately, the *sattvic* way also remains like background music only; and then all becomes an alert Stillness – Pure Bliss.

Gita Gyana 17

- ❑ **17.1:** The texture of attitude and faith determines the success of your endeavour.
- ❑ **17.2:** Pure and unattached undertaking of charity, austerity, service of society and righteous action leads to happiness.
- ❑ **17.3:** *Sattvic* diet is life supportive and mind purifying.
- ❑ **17.4:** *Tamasic* food creates pain, anger and disease.
- ❑ **17.5:** Serve humanity and creation as a whole without selfish intentions, taking it as your duty.
- ❑ **17.6:** Serve and donate with discrimination of the suitability of the receiver, time and place.
- ❑ **17.7:** Pay respect and serve the teacher, the wise man and the knower of Truth.
- ❑ **17.8:** Truthful, pleasant, inoffensive utterance is the *tapas* of speech.
- ❑ **17.9:** *Aum* is Absolute; *Tat* is Universality and *Sat* is Existence. These attributes of Reality must be remembered to experience the Grace of the Supreme in each act.

❑ **18.0:** Nothing can be achieved in life without unshakable faith and confidence in the Eternal Self as well as in yourself.

17. They say faith moves the mountain; the mountain says: "I know this reality."

Chapter 18

Fearless, Doubtless, Perfect and Blissful... You!

In this final chapter of the *Gita*, Arjuna desires to know the essence of the truth of renunciation (*sannyas*) and abandonment (*tyaga*). Krishna not only enlightens Arjuna on these two truths, but also narrates related aspects to finally convince him to fight the Mahabharata war. Krishna says that ceasing all desire-driven activities is renunciation (*sannyas*), while giving up all anxieties about enjoying the fruits of action is abandonment (*tyaga*).

Further, Krishna says that *tyaga* is of three types: an act of sacrifice (service), charity (*daan*), and austerity (*tapas*) must be performed leaving aside attachment and thoughts of reward. This is *sattvic tyaga* (pure abandonment). *Tyaga* of daily duties and obligatory actions against all reasons is *tamasic tyaga* (ignorance, dullness). Giving up obligatory duties because of their painful nature is *rajasic tyaga*; a passionately active person should not be scared of discomfort and pain in an action and, therefore, leaving such an act becomes *rajasic tyaga*.

All beings have to work because it is impossible to give up action completely, but he who gives up the fruits of action is fit to be a relinquisher (*tyagi*). There are three types of fruits of action: unpleasant, pleasant and mixed; they accumulate after death for those who have not given up the longing for rewards of their action. However, for a renunciate (*sannyasi*) who has renounced all desire-driven actions, there is no accumulation of fruits whatsoever. That means *karma* are not generated for the renunciate.

Explaining the deeper implications of 'work', Krishna says that there are five causes for accomplishing all actions: the physical body; the 'doer' (phenomenal ego or *jiva*; the agent), various instruments of perception, various kinds of efforts (organs of actions; vital energy), and Providence (*daivam*, non-human factor, destiny).

But the man of distorted mind and indisciplined understanding thinks himself to be the sole cause as a doer. Such a person does not understand that human actions are the product of Nature. The Self within is only an observer under whose illumination all actions happen. The ego is the veiled spirit and only one of the causes of action. The ego also belongs to *prakriti* (Nature) and not to the Self.

One who is free from egocentric arrogance, with clear thinking and who works as an instrument of the Supreme is not bound even after slaying others for a righteous cause.

Further explaining the impulse that propels activity, Krishna says that Knowledge, the Knowing and the Knower are the threefold cause of action while the sense organs, the action and the doer (ego) make threefold execution of the action.

There are three kinds of knowledge – *sattvic*: One Imperishable Being is seen in all creation; *rajasic*: the multiple nature of Being is seen in different creatures; *tamasic*: not concerned with cause and having no understanding of Reality.

Likewise, work can also be classified into three types – *sattvic* (of goodness; purity): obligatory, performed with a sense of detachment, without love or hate and without desire for fruits. *Rajasic* (passionate and hyperactive): performed with great strain and longing for gratification of one's desires or pride. *Tamasic* (dull, heedless): undertaken through ignorance without thinking of loss, injury or one's own capacity.

Doers are also of three kinds – *sattvic*: free from attachment and egotism, full of resolution, zeal and balanced in success or failure; *rajasic*: passionate, eager for fruits, greedy, of harmful nature, impure and agitated by joy or sorrow. *Tamasic*: imbalanced, vulgar, adamant, dishonest, malicious, lazy, ever complaining and procrastinating.

According to *gunas*, understanding (intellectual capacity) and steadiness (consistency) can be classified into threefold divisions – *sattvic*: by which one knows action and reaction, renunciation, what ought to be done and what not, fear and fearlessness, bondage and freedom. *Rajasic*: by which one holds fast to duty, pleasure and wealth, desiring fruits. *Tamasic*: by which the stupid man does not abandon sleep, fear, grief, depression and arrogance.

Various duties determined by one's nature (*svabhav*) and Natural Law of Being (*swadharma*) are analysed as follows:

Krishna says that all creatures – on earth or in heaven – work under the influence of the three *gunas*. In the fourfold division of Hindu society (based on combinations of various degrees of *gunas*), activities are identified in accordance with the qualities of people and not by birth as has been adopted mistakenly. By worshipping the Supreme through the performance of one's duty, man attains perfection. It is better to perform our duty according to the natural quality of our mind rather than to be engaged in the duty of a contrary nature. One should not abandon the duty suited to one's nature though it may be deficient because all undertakings are enveloped by imperfection.

He further declares that he who has attained perfection reaches *Brahman* – the Eternal. Equipped with pure intellect and clear understanding, controlling the self by firmness, relinquishing objects through sense organs, and abandoning attraction and hatred, dwelling in solitude, eating little, controlling speech, actions and mind, ever engaged in meditation, having abandoned egoism, force, arrogance, desire, anger, possession – such a person is fit to attain *Brahman*.

The next stage of development is explained here – that one who has experienced *Brahman* by practice of the above techniques becomes serene in the Self; he neither grieves nor desires; regards all beings as alike; he obtains superb devotion towards Him, says Krishna. Through devotion he knows the Supreme and merges with Him.

Thus, wisdom, devotion and work go together. As an ultimate caution, Krishna tells Arjuna clearly: "Filled with egoism if you think – 'I will not fight', vain is your resolve, because Nature will compel you (to fight)." Krishna advises Arjuna to surrender to Him with all his being; then by His Grace he will obtain Supreme Peace. Having declared this wisdom – the most secret of the secrets – to Arjuna, Krishna asks him to think about it and to act according to his own discrimination. Arjuna is advised to abandon all egocentric duties, laws, and ethics that are worrying him with regard to the war (killing his kin). "Surrender and act" is the way to salvation and freedom.

Further, Krishna warns that this wisdom is never to be disclosed to a person who is not pure in life, or who has no devotion, no obedience, or who speaks ill of the Supreme. Such negative-minded people can never understand this wisdom and may misuse it. Instead, it should be taught to His devotee and in doing so even the initiator (the teacher) will receive His Grace because such a teacher is dear to God. The study of this secret dialogue, and even listening to it, shall bring happiness and ethical living to a person, opined Krishna.

At the end, Krishna asks Arjuna a direct question – after hearing everything, have all the doubts caused by ignorance been dispelled from Arjuna's mind?

Arjuna answers that Krishna's Grace has dispelled his delusion and now he is determined to act according to the advice given to him. He is ready to fight without a doubt in his mind.

At the end, Sanjay – the narrator of this dialogue to King Dhritarashtra – says that he recalls again and again this Supreme Wisdom of Yoga that was narrated by the King of Yoga, Lord Krishna, Himself. Sanjay was thrilled with astonishment and joy because he was of pure heart.

At the closing phase of the talk, Sanjay tells the king, the father of the Kauravas: "Wherever there is Krishna, the Lord of Yoga, and Partha (Arjuna) – the great archer, I think there will surely be fortune, victory, welfare, and morality."

This is the summary of the eighteenth chapter of the *Gita*, entitled *The Yoga of Liberation by Renunciation*.

The *Gita* teaches us to act, and to act vigorously, in this world. *Sannyas* and *tyaga* do not mean suspending performance and running away from life into the forest. Unfortunately, misinterpretations of the *Gita* have harmed the ignorant masses, leading to inactivity, rampant poverty, fatalism, and lethargic dullness in the name of abandonment of action. On the contrary, the *Gita* emphasises regulating and taming wild, mad, unreasonable desires and fantasies and curbing the agitation of the mind concerning uncertain results of our work. The *Gita* actually takes a positive, dynamic, balanced and composed approach to the problems of life.

Man is an instrument in the hands of Nature, which is the expression of the Supreme. Therefore, man should support the cosmic scheme of creation by serving humanity and the environment through compassion and the least indulgence in self-gratification. These acts ensure peace of mind and happiness.

No doubt, expectation of the fruits of our toil is natural, without which there may be lack of zeal to work. But obsessive focus on rewards creates over-anxiety, nerve-shattering worries, sleepless nights, melancholy, depression and loss of inner calmness leading to dissipation of happiness and drain of energy so essential for proper work. Anxiety about the reward also results in loss of concentration. Therefore, we are advised to leave the outcome to Providence.

Everyone has certain traits, natural attributes, tendencies and intellect bestowed by Nature. At various points of time, although all these three *gunas* – *sattvic, rajasic* and *tamasic* – are present in us, one predominates over the other two.

For getting established in Yoga (of knowledge, action, or devotion) one has to remove all impurities from his mind, speech, and action. For deeper meditation, a cleaning of the intellect-mind-ego is a must. A way is shown here which takes you ultimately to realisation of *Brahman*.

Our aim should be to truthfully analyse and meticulously improve our behaviour from *tamasic* to *rajasic* and ultimately to *sattvic*. This shall free us from the clutches of ignorance and pain and bring the pure light of Consciousness within. We can strive to eradicate our negative tendencies and evolve our talents and inclinations by practice and perseverance. For spiritual perfection, non-attachment and freedom from desires are repeatedly emphasised in the *Gita*. Beside several virtuous attributes and righteous values, these two are said to be the most effective because attachment and desires generate pain, turmoil and unhappiness. For a seeker, their abandonment is essential to make the heart clean and pure.

At the same time, for the worldly person it is highly desirable to strike a balance. Attachment to spouse, children, relations, friends, property, fame and name is apparently natural and required to a certain extent for security and survival in this world. But excess of these is unwarranted. Instead, selfless love, help, support and generosity are positive trends that will replace blind selfish attachment.

Similarly, desires appear to be natural and seemingly help materialistic progress, but unethical, arrogant and corrupt desires are ultimately disastrous, even if you acquire fabulous wealth and power. Again, a sensible balance is needed.

God has graced us with the intelligence to discriminate. In the *Gita*, Lord Krishna has shown us the path to attain liberation from grief and to reach the tranquillity of Pure Consciousness. At the same time, He does not force the decision on you. In the end, Krishna left the decision to Arjuna who had to decide his course of action. Arjuna decided positively and fought with a clear mind and a state of surrender at His feet. Thus, this lesson is important for us to live successfully and happily in this world and to act vigorously.

Wherever there is devotion, faith, virtue, intellect, clear perception, focussed energy, expertise and action, then there is success, victory, prosperity, peace, and freedom and His Grace is sure to descend.

Gita Gyana 18

- ❑ **18.1:** *Sannyas* (renunciation) and *tyaga* (abandonment) are more concerned with mental attitude and toil rather than running away from the challenges of life.
- ❑ **18.2:** Selfless service to humanity as well as to Nature, helping the destitute stand on their feet, self-denial of indulgence – these must be observed ceaselessly.
- ❑ **18.3:** Work with the aim in sight but let not anxiety of the fruit sap your energy even before the goal is attained.
- ❑ **18.4:** Don't think arrogantly that *you* have achieved success and riches; it is an Unseen Factor, a Divine one, which works finally.
- ❑ **18.5:** See the Imperishable in all creation.

- ❑ **18.6:** Resolve to act with zeal but be calm in success or failure.
- ❑ **18.7:** Control the flow of energy and senses through unwavering Yoga of meditation.
- ❑ **18.8:** You can regulate the surroundings, your actions, and circumstances around you to some extent. Destiny, however, remains ever present – but don't be fatalistic to the degree that you become a sloth.
- ❑ **18.9:** Wisdom, devotion and work go together in achieving lasting success and fulfilment.
- ❑ **19.0:** AUM – Fight the battle of life with Krishna's wisdom and Arjuna's might; win the war with demonic circumstances and unhappiness; surrender to the Supreme and meditate on Pure Consciousness. Contemplate on Gita Gyana.

18. Blossom into Beatitude!
Disperse the Fragrance!
Act and earn Fulfilment!
Expand into Infinity!
Merge with Blissful Eternity!

Summary

The Divine Song of the *Gita* is much beyond the realm of the human mind. It cannot be encompassed in the narrow limits of religion or even philosophy. It is a composite of righteous living, balanced thinking, virtuous behaviour, unfolding of the Truth, recognising of the Supreme, a search of the Self within, focus on devotion to finally achieve ultimate salvation and freedom.

The Supreme Intelligence comes to the rescue in our distress only if we surrender in totality; then His Grace shines forth in the darkness of our despair.

All sufferings are caused by longings prompted by our ego; when this is subdued by understanding, knowledge about the Self dawns upon us and the darkness of suffering vanishes. Karma Yoga – to act in the world outside without worrying about the reward that lies in the future and which is not in our hands – can lead us to union with the Absolute. Similarly, when ignorance of our heart is cleaned by knowledge of the Self, Yoga (union) is attained.

To be free in the real sense, one has to be free from greed, fear and anger; one has to control wild desires; one has to contemplate upon Pure Consciousness which is present everywhere; and one must practise meditation. The practice of meditation, along with its cautions and preparatory methods, makes a man perfect and takes him to the highest level of happiness and bliss. By analyses, Reality appears to be veiled by Divine Illusion; in fact, *maya* (illusion) is a superimposition upon Reality. Such a play of *samsar* (*maya* and its ramifications) can be known only through Divine knowledge and wisdom.

It has been asserted in the *Gita* that if one remembers the Infinite at the time of departure from this world, he definitely reaches God; therefore, throughout our life we must remember God so that it becomes effortless to think of Him and to lay our life at His feet at the appropriate time. Thereby, death becomes agonyless. Else, death is painful and traumatic.

The secret of the *Gita* is contained in focussing our mind on the Supreme, in being devoted to Him, in uniting our whole being with Him and making Him our goal. If we 'perceive' Divine glories strewn all around us as well as within ourselves, we shall be able to focus our mind more intensely upon Him during meditation. Therefore, 'perceive' His glory, contemplate and meditate.

The Cosmic Form of the Infinite is beyond human comprehension but we must think about Him as being the Timeless, Spaceless, Beginningless, Endless, Creator, Sustainer and Annihilator of the cosmos, including Brahma and Nature itself. He is Time Unlimited. Pure love and devotion to the Infinite God-Principle make our life complete and dissolve limitations. Devotion to Him and love for His creation in which His spark shines will take you to the highest plane of existence.

It has been advocated that knowledge of *prakriti* and *Purusha* leads to rediscovery of Pure Awareness within. The Self within is veiled by the qualities of *prakriti*; otherwise, it is Pure Consciousness. Once we discover the Self, the ego vanishes and Realisation dawns.

While living in the world, we must try to upgrade our *sattvic gunas*, which in association with pure intellect (making it *sattvic buddhi*) reflects the Supreme more brilliantly within us. The Highest Spirit – *Purushottama* – is Infinite Consciousness; It illumines all – whatever exists or does not exist!

In case of doubt about action, let the scripture be your guide as an authority in taking a decision – what to do and what not to do. Strive hard to imbibe divine traits and to discard devilish ones.

False values in life are to be renounced and righteous ones to be evolved. This will lead us to the higher plane of existence. Wherever there is discriminative intellect and quietude of mind, wherever there is vigorous action, power and dexterity in performance, there is prosperity, victory, happiness and justice.

In this world, with multitude of ups and downs, one must strike a balance of the mind. Work and action are prime factors to succeed. Lethargic fatalism is negative. Your *karma* makes your destiny; therefore, skilfully steer your *karma*, and destiny will take care of itself. Vigorous performance with expertise (planning, material, techniques, supports, etc) keeps you on the path to success although one unknown factor always remains, which determines the final achievement. Surrender this factor unto the Almighty. Do not get agitated about it. He will take care of it if you leave this unto Him. This is not escapist fatalism but sensible practicality because you cannot control the future.

Poverty is a sin and negative fatalism a crime. Work hard, produce wealth with honesty, fight problems with a calm mind, live a full life, and know the relation between yourself, the world and the Supreme. Be fearless, pure and firm, without pride, calm in ups-and-downs, honest, disciplined, compassionate, and helpful to the destitute. Other traits of wisdom in life will creep in!

Energy is immortal; it can't be destroyed. It changes its form into another type of energy or synthesises into matter and expresses itself at the other plane of time-space. Likewise, matter maintains equilibrium with energy. When we depart from this world, the spark of Eternal Energy leaves our body. The body decays and merges with gross elements, yet its existence continues in some form of energy because matter and energy balance each other. Eternal Energy (the soul) migrates along with the subtle energy of our *karma* to another womb or another plane of existence.

Then, who dies? The *atman* is immortal. So there is nothing to grieve about!

Yoga is the best way to evolve oneself – physically, mentally, emotionally and spiritually; it is not a religion to be imposed. It is a tried and tested natural system to improve various facets of our personality and focus the mind on the Supreme through concentration. Ultimately, everything dissolves and only a Dynamic Silence remains. *You are That.*

The Absolute has no form, shape or limit. He is neither existent nor non-existent. Yet He is present in all. Therefore, do not harm any creatures or Nature.

AUM is not a dogmatic sound or a symbol of any particular belief. Its echo can be understood in the sound of the Big Bang when Time and Space were created. Thus, AUM represents the Absolute; else, how can we visualise Him? However, one can choose any other sound or symbol of his conviction.

But the Absolute is much beyond the Big Bang! Meditate upon the symbolic sound and say AUM, because our mind needs a substratum, or a 'vehicle', to maintain its concentration; thereafter, that vehicle may as well be left behind when you attain Pure Consciousness, Supreme Awareness, Dynamic Silence and the Truth!

'Perceive' the glory of God in flowers, the sun, the moon, the sky, the breeze, the smile of a child, love, birth, death, and the brilliance of the mind and in Nature all around you. Thus will you experience His Splendour!

Appendix I

Meditation: An Integral Part of Yoga

Yoga means to *join*. On the mental level, Yoga implies control of circling waves of the mind (i.e., *chitta*: the mental, intellectual, egotistical field of our personality). In the spiritual context, Yoga is that practice which *unites* the spirit of the seeker with the Supreme. This Divine knowledge and its practice bring the being in direct 'union' with Pure Consciousness. It is a nonpareil experience that releases a person from agitation and unhappiness, connects with the quietude of mind and ushers in Bliss. It brings fulfilment in life through all the realms of multiple dimensions. Is this not the ultimate aim of our life?

In totality, the subject of Yoga is extensive and vast. An immense contribution has been made on its multiple facets since time immemorial. Therefore, in this brief essay only an outline is given in conjunction with the teachings of the *Gita*. However, some details on meditation based on the experience of learned sages and seekers have been added. In fact, the *Gita* in itself is a complete compendium of Yoga.

The ways of Yoga are varied, based on the energy field through which unification of the Self with the Reality is sought. Some of the main fields are:

- Yoga of Devotion (Bhakti Yoga)
- Yoga of Action (Karma Yoga)
- Yoga of Knowledge (Gyana Yoga)
- Yoga of Mantra (Mantra Yoga)
- Yoga of Merger (Laya Yoga)
- Yoga of Physical Empowerment (Hatha Yoga)
- Royal Yoga (Raj Yoga)

Each one of these practices has a different goal as well as methodology but basically all have a common direction because at the higher plane of achievements they merge with each other and march thereafter on a common path of unity with the Self.

In other words, extensive fields of worldly performance as well as intellectual activities are covered under Yoga if accomplished with single-minded concentration, a non-agitated mind, selfless attitude and purity of the heart. The ultimate aim is an attempt for merging with Pure Consciousness through the body (unattached action), mind (control of thought flow), intellect (Divine knowledge), and ego (sublimation). In the *Gita*, Krishna has defined all the main realms of Yoga.

Yoga of Devotion: It comprises total surrender, with love and devotion at the altar of the Personal or Impersonal God, the Almighty. Purity of heart, an egoless state of mind, continual practice, total imbibing of Reality into our existence, and unwavering faith and dissolution of I-ness and my-ness in the Absolute are essentials for the Yoga of Devotion.

This Yoga is most suited for the man of loving emotion and tenderness towards creation. The Yoga of Devotion dissolves the limits of our self-sense and helps us merge with the Eternal Energy.

Yoga of Action: It requires acts and performance in the world outside, without attachment, anxiety and desire for the fruits of action. Expectation of rewards for our work is to be laid at His feet. This keeps you free from worries about the future. It is the best Yoga for a man of action but the act should be performed without passion. The Yoga of Action helps in exhausting remnant tendencies of the past existence. When the desire for vigorous action is exhausted, the mind becomes quiet, serene and non-agitated, and ready for higher states of consciousness.

Yoga of Knowledge: It comprises right understanding of Creation, the Creator, the Cosmos, and life and death. This is Divine Knowledge. It ushers into the realm of all life, the Imperishable Lord, the Truth and the Reality. It is to be comprehended that the Supreme is Beginningless and Endless, Immutable; the rest is His manifestation. Pure Consciousness is an observer while His Nature appears to be active.

A complete surrender through intellectual practice is called for in the Yoga of Knowledge. For this, a clean heart and unshakable sharp knowledge is required. "Who am I?" should be enquired continuously. Such an analysis will calm down all your uneasy queries about God, Nature and the Self and peace will descend within. This will lead to union with the Great Silence.

Yoga of Mantra: It is a technique by which a name, a sound, a mantra, or a metre is repeated often, with thoughts of the Almighty. The mantra is chanted mentally or with the help of a rosary. In due course of time, thoughts become sublime and our concept of the God that we believe in becomes firm and single-pointed. One may experience ecstasy and bliss, which are the vehicles for higher levels of consciousness.

This is a part of Japa Yoga (repetition of His name while keeping Him in mind) and should be performed regularly with unshakable faith, and without any desire.

Yoga of Merger (Laya Yoga): The basic principle of this Yoga rests on the concept that the human body is constituted exactly like the universe. By subduing gross sheaths of the body, this can be established at any plane of existence. By practice of this Yoga, the *Kundalini* (the serpent power of the energy; the creative *Shakti*) that lies dormant, coiled at the end of the spinal cord, can be invoked. The cord, the connecting brain, as well as their surrounding regions in the body can be used as the pathway for Kundalini when it is made active and uncoiled by concentration of thoughts at that spot. It then creeps upwards crossing six nodal points of energy, from base to the top of the path within the vertebral column through the nerve-plexus within and reaches the forehead where it merges (*Laya*) with the Lord of Creation.

This unification of *Shiva* and *Shakti* is brought about by persistent performance of Laya Yoga. But it cannot be practised without the guidance of an accomplished guru.

Yoga of Physical Empowerment (Hatha Yoga): It requires various exercises, postures of the body (*asanas*), breath control (*Pranayam*), and severe austerity of the body and mind. There is a vast field of methodical performance of physical manipulations in this Yoga and it should therefore be practised under the guidance of an expert. Hatha Yoga streamlines and channels the vital energies of the body.

In theory, Hatha Yoga involves control of the gross body by various postures, and that of the subtle body (the *chitta* or life energy) to merge with the Eternal.

Royal Yoga (Raj Yoga): It comprises Yoga of the mind and will power. The meditation – also known as Dhyana Yoga – is an integral component of Raj Yoga. The aim of Raj Yoga, through meditation, is to remove various mental obstructions and to make the body as well as the mind befitting and disciplined for achieving union with the Divine. To regulate desires in the direction of the union with the Self and to concentrate faculties of the mind for the ultimate merger is the aim of meditation. The basics of Raj Yoga reveal that the mind (along with intellect and ego) binds man, yet a disciplined mind can liberate him as well. Therefore, purification of these components removes ignorance and helps in Realisation.

Royal Yoga is said to be the best amongst all the Yogas. Of course, it best suits the person with high mental faculties, with low chances for physical involvement in the world of indulgence and an inclination towards righteous thinking.

Raj Yoga includes some characteristics of each type of Yoga, at one stage or the other, and hence it is termed Royal Yoga.

Meditation

A person who develops a disciplined mind through regulated, unattached, unselfish desires could control the materialistic world of objects, superpowers and the animate multitudes with their powers. It has been experienced by accomplished Yogis that if one is victorious over the mind he can win the world! An intense concentration of the mind (*chitta*: in a wider sense, the mind means thought flow, the intellect, our heart and the I-ness) on a particular object or concept reveals its hidden characteristics and invokes its inherent power. Ultimately, by constant practice, the seeker may be empowered with supernatural energy and extraordinary knowledge.

The basic techniques of meditation are contained in making the mind introverted and fixing it in Dynamic Silence, removing turbulent obstructions in the thinking pattern, and diverting the energy thus generated through concentration towards our *atman* – the Self, the Divine Spark, within us. Prolonged practice of meditation will reveal that our *atman* (the soul), which has been veiled by the qualities (good or evil) of Nature or *prakriti*, is a pure, immortal ray of Pure Consciousness. The Absolute is not different from our Self and we do not have to go outside in search of Him. This, the Eternal Energy of Consciousness, is present in each and every aspect of creation.

Before undertaking meditation, it is mandatory to make the mind clean and the body fit in all respects. An impure mind or diseased body cannot succeed in concentration and contemplation. Therefore, including preparatory methods, Raj Yoga has been structured on eight organs (or parts, steps, components, planes, levels, etc), which are to be done step-wise up to the culmination point. Meditation is the seventh level of experience.

These eight levels are:

1. Yam
2. Niyam
3. Aasan
4. Pranayam
5. Pratyahar
6. Dharna
7. Dhyana (meditation)
8. Samadhi

The first four steps are common with Hatha Yoga, from amongst which the first two include all the major areas of mental discipline and cleansing of the thought pattern. They are universal in nature and mostly shared by all religious philosophies of the world. The third and the fourth, *Aasan* and *Pranayam,* are meant to develop physical agility and strength by regulating the life-sustaining breathing systems.

The first four organs are thus concerned with mental uplift and physical fitness. They are known as *Bahirang* (exterior) components. The fifth component – *Pratyahar,* a connecting link – is a jump from the body level to the higher mind level of *Dharna-Dhyana-Samadhi* (*Antrang*) states of escalation and, ultimately, the exalted bliss.

Pratyahar comprises a diversion of the mind from outer objects and then fixing it on the inner object, or the ideal, or the concept; in other words, it is a control of thoughts and then their desired steering according to our aim on to the ideal of meditation. *Pratyahar,* the total control of the mind, connects *Bahirang* (exterior) and *Antrang* (interior) components of Raj Yoga.

Thereafter, the sixth stage of the flight is *Dharna,* which comprises unwavering concentration on one point or an object of choice. The seventh stage is meditation – *Dhyana,* awareness full of silence. And the last one is *Samadhi,* the merger of all in the One. There is none else except Pure Consciousness on achieving *Samadhi*.

Structure of Meditation and Other Components

The one who is unattached to desires and faithfully strives to achieve freedom through steadiness is the real expedient of Yoga.

The waves of the mind in the ordinary state change every moment but at the culmination of meditation (in *Samadhi*), the waves attain unified silence. The mind can be controlled by the practice of *Ashtang* (the eight-fold organs of Raj Yoga) and then by intellectual discrimination of the Real and the unreal. So also, with a mental attitude of detachment from the world of objects, relationships and happenings a single-pointedness of mind can be achieved. Faith and persistent efforts are supportive. The *Gita* is the true Guide, or Guru, for all these undertakings.

The eight-fold components of Raj Yoga are:

1. YAM: Non-violence, truth, not stealing, continence and non-accumulation constitute *Yam*.

- i. **Non-violence:** *Ahimsa* is a very powerful aspect of Yoga. Not to kill any being (e.g., to be a vegetarian), or not to trouble anyone or even the self, non-injury (i.e., not committing self-torture through rituals or anger) by way of action, speech, or thoughts. In spirit, non-violence as an unselfish way has a different connotation and killing in war to protect a righteous cause or awarding punishment for establishing the Law of Life is not negated. Non-violence is not cowardice. On the contrary, it is a brave, strong value of abeyance from unjust killings. If practised sincerely, other beings and creatures coming in contact with the practitioner also abjure violence.
- ii. **Truth (*Satya*):** Non-covetousness in thoughts, words, or deeds; not to lie; to remain silent where an inevitable situation arises; to speak as the mind or the sense organs have felt it without deceit or double talk. Truth will prevail if there is no selfishness.

However, where the Law of Being (*dharma*) is in jeopardy, the opposite is not negated. Truth generates moral power and strength of conviction. If practised fully, a pronouncement of the practitioner becomes a 'truth'.

iii. **Not stealing (*Asteya*):** In the strict sense, it means not to take somebody's possession without his permission. Not to steal means even not to usurp somebody's right. The practice of *Asteya* reduces desires for worldly objects and keeps one free from a guilty conscience. *Asteya* strengthens your credentials and you become the recipient of all that is 'desired'.

iv. **Continence (*Brahmacharya*):** Perfect chastity in thought, word and deed; besides abstinence from illegal and corrupt indulgence in sensual relationships, continence is said to be established if the thoughts, senses and the body are not involved in any sort of unchaste gratification. Exposure to sensuous literature, exhibits or fantasy saps your vital energy, which is needed for concentration of the mind. A disciplined life increases your power and influence in all walks of life. But any self-inflicting, unnatural, degrading and cruel abstinence is not implied in *Brahmacharya*. Conservation of our life energy and the faculty of the mind is its main aim, which otherwise is dissipated by indulgence in bodily pleasures. Leading a socially acceptable, pious family life for progeny is not against *Brahmacharya*, if logically regulated and disciplined.

v. **Non-accumulation (*Aparigraha*):** Non-receiving of gifts. There is no end to materialistic luxuries in the world and in modern times, everyday newer and more attractive objects are floated in the market. Consumerism brings no satiation but only creates jealousy, competition, inferiority complex, gluttony and pain. The only way to satisfaction is to keep our needs within limits and to avoid superfluous things.

Such a practice will bring lasting happiness and harmony in life.

In a wider sense, *Aparigraha* includes non-accumulation of luxury related to sound, touch, vision, taste, and smell – the ill-conceived wild demands of the sense organs. *Aparigraha* generates non-attachment. However, it does not mean living in scarcity and in want for basic requirements, and with the need for shelter, health, safety, education and basic necessities. The warning is against indulgence in sense gratification without check, which makes you a hollow creature in the end. Instead, fill yourself with the pleasure of compassion, help for the needy, love and charity.

The five disciplines described above are pure qualities that are to be mastered at the first step – the *Yama* – for the upward journey. If you start with one, the others will follow one by one.

2. NIYAM: Purity, contentment, austerity, study of the scripture and devotion to the Divine.

i. **Purity (*Suchi*):** Everybody knows the significance of outer cleanliness of the body, our dwelling, our surrounding and the environment, including air, water, earth, etc. The abandonment of selfishness amounts to cleanliness of behaviour and conduct, while negation of corrupt and unfair earning leads to purity of materials that we consume to maintain our body functions. All these constitute exterior cleansing.

However, interior purity is more urgent as there proliferates a clutter of self-sense, attachment, likes and dislikes, jealousy, hatred, fear, greed, lust, and anger. Unless we make our inner self clean, chaste and free from these cobwebs, nothing can be achieved – neither peace nor our goal. The practice of *Suchi* shall make our personality transparent, clean and auspicious.

ii. **Contentment (*Santosh*):** The practice of contentment involves keeping the mind in balance and equipoise in the face of opposites of contradictory situations – comfort-pain, profit-loss, honour-dishonour, fame-infamy, favour-disfavour, etc. To be contented is a powerful asset of nature. Discontent generates non-satiable thirst for materialistic possessions.

However, it should not be taken as a negative trait of satisfaction against progress, which may otherwise produce lethargy and inaction resulting in poverty and failure even in a justified pursuit. Act you must, earn you should by righteous and incorrupt means but whatever comes to you by way of intelligent planning and hard, sincere work, it must give you a sense of fulfilment, rather than dissatisfaction, even if it falls short of your expectations. *Santosh* makes you a complete person.

iii. **Austerity (*Tapas*):** It means observing a *sattvic*, pure, enlightened way of following *swadharma* (law of ethics, virtues and humanity; service to others) even if you have to bear inconvenience, difficulties, or discomfort of the body or mind to some extent. Of course, the cause for *tapas* must be humanitarian, and for justice and compassion rather than selfishness and fanaticism. *Tapas* 'melts' your being and filters impurities, bringing out pure 'gold' of virtue. It gives the practitioner an immense power of mind, normally not achieved by other means.

iv. **Study of Scripture (*Swadhyay*):** It includes study, and contemplation thereupon, of literature concerning religions, humanity, morals, Creation, Nature, the God-Principle, Self, philosophy and allied aspects of enlightenment. The garbage of information with no consequence for spiritual progress should be minimised. However, professional knowledge and study for students are not negated because that comes under the purview of *Swadhyay*.

In reading the scripture, there should be no bias against different religions, cultures, civilisations, philosophies and concepts because knowledge of virtuous values is more or less common in all fields of ethical learning. A wider study widens your view and takes you forward on the path to realisation.

v. **Devotion to the Divine (*Ishwara Pranidhan*):** The Absolute is One without a second. The universe is His manifestation expressed through Cosmic Intelligence – *Ishwara* or the Supreme. All is created, sustained and dissolved merely by His expression that functions through Nature – also a creation of the Supreme. Contemplation, devotion and love to the Personal God (with Form; your mental reflection), or to the Impersonal God (Formless, Pure Awareness) and making Him the whole and sole of your life is *Pranidhan*. The Supreme is expressed in every iota of Creation; therefore, help and support to the animate and inanimate encompasses His worship. *Pranidhan* is like a pleasant bath in the waters of bliss and love. It gives peace and everlasting liberation.

The ten ingredients of *Yam* and *Niyam* outlined above generate positive energy in your being. Any act against these produces a multitude of anti-life, negative field of energy because they multiply in geometrical ratio in conjunction with the mind and the ego and also by other persons associated with your negative actions.

3. AASAN (Posture of the body): To remain seated comfortably without the slightest movement of the body is known as *Aasan*. During meditation, one generally sits on the ground with crossed legs, putting the right foot on the thigh of the left leg (folded) and the left foot on the thigh of the right leg (folded); this is known as *Padmasan* (the Lotus Posture). The other seating posture is *Sukhasan* (Comfortable Posture) in which only one foot is placed over the thigh of the other leg (folded), which rests on the ground.

Besides these, there are numerous other *aasanas* performed by manipulating the upper and lower limbs, the trunk and the head in various complicated ways; such postures are part of Hatha Yoga and said to open energy channels in the body.

However, for the purpose of meditation, our aim is to understand that sitting on the ground or on a low platform with folded legs in an easy position makes a posture suitable for *Dhyana*. One must not sit on the bare, hard floor. It must be covered with a moderately soft mattress or a folded blanket. The seat must not be too low or too high. The seeker should be neither hungry nor overfull during meditation.

While in posture, the vertebral column of the meditator must remain erect, straight and aligned with the head in the vertical position; the trunk of the body and the head should be at a right angle to the formation of the folded legs. The hands must be kept comfortably on the lap. The eyes should be softly closed – neither wide open nor tightly shut; the mental 'eye' or focus of the mind must be fixed between the eyebrows or on the tip of the nose. Actual fixing of the eyes on these points would be too strenuous, hence only our mental 'eye' should be focused on this region.

The rhythm of breathing must be natural, slow, and effortless. Relax every joint and every muscle of the body. There should be no stiffness, tightness or forcible pressure, voluntary or involuntary, on any part of the body. Practise this repeatedly everyday. Thus one will become proficient in it.

One must sit motionless in an *aasan* for about half an hour, or even more. The body and mind both must be motionless, calmed down by practice. To attain this, the place for meditation should be an isolated corner in the house, or it may be outside in an exceptional case, in which case the process can be altered to suit the situation. The place of meditation must have very dim lights; without noise or sound disturbances and interference by anybody. Almost all the senses – eyes, nose, ears, tongue and skin – should be mentally switched-off, as far as possible. The mind plays a major role in cutting the connection off from the outer and inner worlds.

4. PRANAYAM: This means regulating the breathing pattern. Pranayam itself is a vast field of learning that should be learnt from an adept. For our purpose, it must be taken in a simplified, non-strenuous, effortless and non-taxing manner.

Breathing in is known as 'inhalation'; breathing out is 'exhalation'; the control of both is Pranayam. Systematic regulation of the breath helps in keeping the body fit and the mind in concentration.

According to the scripture, Pranayam is mainly of eight types. However, for our purpose we shall deal only with the main Pranayam (control of life energy), with few words on two supportive techniques.

Before undertaking actual Pranayam, *naadi shodhan* may be performed for cleansing of energy paths. Seated in the *aasan,* perfectly calm and steady, by closing the right nostril with the thumb of the right hand, the air is to be drawn within slowly through the left nostril, as deep as comfortably possible; then without holding the air within, it should be exhaled slowly through the right nostril by closing the left nostril with the little finger and the ring-finger of the right hand. This should be repeated by alternating the nostrils for inhaling and exhaling. This process of *naadi shodhan* should be performed up to seven times in one sitting, each set of performance at least twice a day – one in the morning and one in the evening. After two or three months, one feels lighter in the body as lethargy is cleared.

The Technique of Pranayam: Inhaling is called *poorak,* holding of the breath within is known as *kumbhak* and exhaling is *rechak.* First, while sitting in the *aasan,* with the thumb of the right hand the right nostril is closed and air is inhaled slowly through the left nostril, mentally counting up to eight; this becomes *poorak*. Then by closing both the nostrils, the right nostril with the thumb and the left with the ring finger and the little finger together, the air should be held within the lungs counting mentally up to 32; this becomes *kumbhak*.

Thereafter, by releasing the thumb, the breath should be exhaled slowly through the right nostril (the left nostril remaining closed), counting mentally up to 16; this becomes *rechak*. Now alternating, this process is to be repeated by starting *poorak* through the right nostril.

The duration for each phase, *poorak, kumbhak* and *rechak*, is to be adjusted in the ratio of 1:4:2, according to the comfort and convenience of the practitioner. Also, instead of counting numbers, one may mentally pronounce the eternal sound AUM, the symbol of Eternal Truth. However, any other short name or sound of the seeker's own choice or faith may be thought of. Even rhythmic, soft music helps, as it produces a flow of sequential melody.

Pranayam should be done with ease, without strain or force of any sort. Twice a day with five to ten cycles of *poorak, kumbhak* and *rechak* each time is a fair practice. One must be seated in the *aasan*, perfectly relaxed and tranquil. The place where Pranayam is performed should be airy, pleasant and properly ventilated.

Some seekers practise *Sheetali Pranayam* (cool and facile energy flow) for making the body healthy. In this, the air is inhaled as deeply as possible, but slowly through the mouth by making both lips round, as if one is whistling; then keeping the breath within for a certain time, comfortably, by closing the mouth and, thereafter, exhaling through both nostrils. There is no alternation of inhaling or exhaling involved here; therefore, the same process of inhaling through the mouth, holding within and exhaling through both the nostrils is repeated. The *Sheetali Pranayam* could be performed twice or thrice a day with five to seven minutes duration each time.

Space constraints do not permit description of the other types of Pranayam or varied breathing exercises. However, the main Pranayam described above is the most recognised and widely practised.

5. PRATYAHAR: The senses and their faculties are detached and withdrawn from their fields of activities and they are then controlled by the *chitta* (mind, intellect, ego and heart). Here, the seeker must practise holding his desires, check them from wandering, and focus likewise on the determined concept or symbol. He mentally cuts himself off from the outer world, therefore *Pratyahar* is done only while sitting in meditation and not while performing actions outside it.

By continuous practice, the seeker brings the senses under his command – a state necessary for meditation.

6. DHARNA: To fix the *chitta* in a particular object, field or concept is known as *Dharna*. The object could be gross or subtle, exteriorly placed or conceptualised within. It could be a Personal God, a symbol, an idol, an image, a flame, the sun, the moon, or the Impersonal, Formless, Absolute. A pin-pointed fixation of *chitta* in such a realm of the aim, for as long as one can, prepares the seeker for the next state of achievement, which is meditation.

7. DHYANA (Meditation): *Dhyana* is the seventh step of Yoga through which the seeker enters the transcendental state of the Self. A continuous uninterrupted flow of *chitta* (mind and its attributes) on the object of worship or other field leads to meditation. Seated in the posture of the *aasan*, practised in an isolated place, relaxing the body, focusing the mind at the tip of the nose or the centre of the eyebrows, comfortably and lightly closing the eyes, watching the rhythm of breathing mentally, without movement, observing wandering thoughts but not being involved in them, one concentrates on the 'object' of his meditation. The seeker forgets the world outside as well as inside.

The first six practices help in meditation and even while doing them one may enter the seventh, meditation, without much effort. Obviously the intensive practice of the preparatory six steps is important without which lasting success may elude the seeker.

The multiple concepts of meditation are, however, based on the foundation erected on one principle, i.e., the Truth Principle is One; it is Pure Consciousness that pervades all; only the purified intellect, functioning in Dynamic Silence can experience the Truth – the Supreme. During the alertness of Silence, the Reality comes face-to-face with the seeker. To achieve this state of mind, one must concentrate on one point of his 'object', or watch the thoughts as a noncommittal observer; or even to seek Silence between two thoughts or intermittently between two pronouncements of AUM, a mantra or any sound of one's choice.

Thus, from amongst several methods, the seeker must adopt one that suits him best. Mostly, concentrating or 'watching' a point, a mental sound, a symbol, an idol, or the Formless are preferred. The sound of AUM is recommended the most by the realised, since it is the primordial resonance.

The place for meditation should be clean and peaceful. The duration of meditation should be preferably half an hour in the early morning and then in the evening. As a rule, you must not eat too much nor be frugal in eating. You must also not sleep too much or too little.

It is, no doubt, difficult to control the mind, yet by negation, thoughts are discarded one by one. Ultimately, Silence descends. Visualising your body merging with space and your being melting into the Universe helps you forget the existence of your body itself. A blissful state arises when you transcend the mind. Then, His Grace showers upon you!

8. SAMADHI: Through meditation you enter *Samadhi*, where only you and your Ideal remain. None else. In the end, all duality dissolves and your existence merges with Silence. Neither you nor your symbol, nor even sound exists there. This is the nonpareil experience, a Supreme Ecstasy and realisation of the Self.

When complete success in Yoga is achieved, it is said that the seeker acquires supernatural powers as blessings. But one is warned not to use them for selfish purposes, else there will be disaster and the entire effort will be in vain.

In Conclusion

Yoga, as a whole, is a positive practice for realisation of powers of the body, mind and the intellect. In the above account, only a general version has been given to suit most persons who are engaged in worldly affairs yet wish to 'evolve'.

Meditation is the most crucial component of Yoga for achieving serenity of mind and to inculcate calm and composed behaviour. This leads to stable happiness. The other steps prior to meditation purify the mind of the seeker and cultivate virtues that support meditation. For example, one cannot succeed in meditation if he is untruthful, cruel and corrupt.

In the *Gita*, the King of Yoga Himself taught the fundamentals of various paths of Yoga. As such, every concept in the *Gita* is Yoga in itself. The virtues and traits of purity are ideal. One may practise as much as possible and then enter into the Silence and Awareness of meditation during the prescribed time. Come out of it and act vigorously in the world. You will be a changed person.

Yoga and meditation are not confined to any religion or faith. Even the *Gita* does not preach any narrow religious thought. In one form or the other, this knowledge of Yoga has been practised and advised by all the founders of great religions of the world. It is a science of the human mind and body with an aim to achieve Oneness (Union) with the Self, the Supreme.

In the following pages, two tables are given:

1. *Just Start Meditation;*
2. *Enter the Dynamic Silence.*

To begin with, practise the first one for about a year and then take up the second one also – for the rest of your life. The detailed bearing is given in the *Gita*. Further reading suggested at the end of this book can well be of help for those who wish to swim in Celestial Waters!

Table 1

Just Start Meditation

Practise Non-violence: Try not to hurt or inflict pain on other beings by bodily damage, insult or dishonour. Be strictly vegetarian. Do not disturb the environment.

Practise Contentment: To be content does not mean to be inactive. Pseudo-satisfaction leads to lethargy and fatalism. Contentment is a deep sense of fulfilment. Work hard, earn a lot and be content!

Practise the *Aasan*: Sit silently in an isolated place; close your eyes; take easy, deep breaths, watch the pattern of inhalation and exhalation. Don't move and keep your mind quiet. Keep fit by healthy living.

Withdraw: Watch the wild dance of thoughts; it is all a clutter. Just 'watch' and smile at them. Most thoughts are ridiculous.

Be a Commander: Control the senses; control the roller-coaster of thoughts about business, work, sensuality, relationships, wealth, power, fame and progeny; calm them down during the half an hour sitting and talk to God.

Non-flickering Flame: Let the flame of the mind not flicker. Fix it on the Ideal of your meditation.

Switch-off Noise: Try to remain in deep silence. If the noise of fluttering ideas and oscillation of thoughts disturb you, bring the mind back to the point of the 'aim' and pacify the mind like the way you do a child.

Think: Who am I? For what purpose have I come into this world? Where lies stable happiness? What will remain in the end? What is the aim of my life?

Fulfil Yourself: Be compassionate; share your earnings sensibly with the genuinely needy; help the destitute and Nature and serve creation. You shall be fulfilled.

Be Free: Freedom means liberation, salvation, *moksha*. Break the bondage and create your own time and space – reserved only for you and no one else. Be liberated; live fully, act vigorously. Let Divine traits shine forth through you – and then be in Bliss.

Table 2

Enter the Dynamic Silence

1. Be Established in YAM: Practise non-violence (don't kill, don't injure, be vegetarian); practise truth in all walks of life; do not usurp others' rights or things; control unruly desires; practise non-indulgence in sensuality; and do not accumulate useless objects, information or thoughts; abandon extreme consumerism.

2. Be Established in NIYAM: Be pure in thought and clean in body; abandon addiction; feel fulfilled, not empty; renounce the extraneous; study and contemplate upon the Truth; surrender to the Almighty; He is the Mother and Father of all Creation; you are a nonentity.

3. Keep Fit: Walking, exercising, proper and *sattvic* eating, balanced living and non-agitation keep one fit. Then practise the *aasan* meticulously.

4. Regulate Energy Flows: Practise simple Pranayam; adapt according to your capacity or breathe deeply in rhythm. Don't overdo things and don't strain.

5. Withdraw: Pull out all the five senses from their fields; regulate thoughts through concentration or simple observation; be a commander of your inner self, of your senses – including the ego.

6. Fixation: Concentrate the rays of your *chitta* on a point; gross tendencies will burn just like concentrated rays pass through a biconvex lens and burn paper. Like a flow of oil, keep your *chitta* unwavy.

7. Meditation: Concentrate on AUM. This is the symbol of the Primordial Echo – Pure Consciousness. If not, focus on a symbol, a name, or a concept of your choice; or a mantra; or on the Sun – a manifestation of the Eternal

Energy which we can see and feel directly. Be empty and He will fill and fulfil you.

8. Dynamic Silence: By practice, your 'Object' of meditation and 'you' will remain – the rest will evaporate! Then ultimately both will dissolve and Total Awareness will flow. This is transcendental *Samadhi* – the Dynamic Silence.

Act: When you come out of meditation, work vigorously but do not be too anxious about the fruits of your toil. It will create turmoil and your meditation will not yield results!

Be Humane: Love all beings and love Nature. The Supreme is present everywhere. Strike a balance; don't be an extremist; be humane and compassionate; love and live a full life. His Grace will descend upon you!

Appendix II

1. Cosmic Time and Pure Awareness

A wheel is rotating – round, around,
A conch shell is blowing – ever resound!

Generation... Brahma
Organisation... Vishnu
Dissolution... Shiva
G-O-D of universe, immanent
Or, A-U-M, the Creation vibrant!

The wheel in continuity,
The self-generative velocity,
Is it the force of Destiny?
Or the Destiny of Eternity?
The one who could be known,
Or could not be known –
Trans-mental.

Whatever is, it IS
The Being – the IS – Elemental
This is Awareness, Pure
This is ever-resounding, of yore

The One Self – aware,
The Awareness of Silence,
Or the Silence of Awareness?

In the Whirl of Time and Alertness,
In the Circularity and Waves of Silence,
I am the Enlightened One –
The Self-illumined,
The Observer of the Truth, that –
A Wheel of Cosmic Time is rotating,
A Conch of Awareness resounding!

2. Who Am I?

Life – an unknown spark of light –
The darkness before the spark,
The darkness beyond the spark,
    Brilliant moment, the life
    Unknown moment, the life
Its abode is not in sight!

Galaxies, stars, moons, earths
With varied forms and shapes,
All illumined by the Self –
Synchronisation with Eternity,
But a ray of His Totality!

A cosmic fireball
Air, Water, Space –
Cell-by-cell life evolved
From amoeba to Adam,
Phenomenon – conceived?
A drop in the oceanic expanse
So is life's existence.

Who am I?
From where have I come?
What is tomorrow?

An earthen pot, deep within the water,
The water inside me, outside me –
The pot is broken, O Water! I am within Thee
From Great-Void to Great-Void
The unmanifested, Formless, Unified.
The life, an unknown ray of His Radiance
Think of the Total Brilliance!

Selected Reading

1. Brunton, P. (1994): *The Hidden Teachings Beyond Yoga*. Pp. 365. B.I. Publication Pvt Ltd, New Delhi.
2. Capra, F. (1975): *The Tao of Physics*. Pp. 412. Flamingo, Hammersmith, London W 6/B.
3. Chinmayananda, Swami (1992): *The Holy Gita* – Commentary. Pp. 1,186. Central Chinmaya Mission Trust, Sandipani Sadhnalaya, Powai Park Drive, Bombay.
4. Choubey, G.K. (1995): *Atmanubhuti*. Pp. 368 (in Hindi). Gayatri Prakashan, 15, Patrakar Colony, Ratlam.
5. Dalal, A.S. (1997): *Growing Within* – Selections from the Works of Sri Aurobindo and the Mother (a compilation). Pp. 192. Sri Aurobindo Ashram, Pondicherry.
6. Garde, L.N. & Poddar, H.P. (Eds) – (1997): *Yogank Kalayan:* A collection of varied articles on Yoga (in Hindi). Pp. 161. Gita Press, Gorakhpur.
7. Goyanka, H.K. (1983): *Patanjalyogadarshan* – A commentary. Pp. 184. Gita Press, Gorakhpur.
8. Goyanka, J.D. (1995): *Srimad Bhagwad Gita*. Pp. 607. A commentary (in Hindi). Gita Press, Gorakhpur.
9. Hawking, S. (1987): *A Brief History of Time*. Pp. 211. Bantam Books, Cambridge.
10. Prabhavananda, Swami & Isherwood, C. (1999): *Patanjali Yoga Sutras* – A New Commentary. Pp. 167. Sri Ramkrishna Math, Mylapur, Madras.
11. Radhakrishnan, S. (1956): *The Bhagvad Gita:* A Commentary. Pp. 383. George Allen & Unvin Ltd, Ruskin House Museum Street, London.
12. Rama, Swami (1996): *Sacred Journey – Living Purposefully and Dying Gracefully*. Pp. 126. Himalayan International Institute of Yoga Science & Philosophy. Malviya Nagar, New Delhi.

13. Satprakashananda, Swami (1976): *Meditation: Its Process, Practice and Culmination*. Pp. 264. Sri Ramkrishna Math, Mylapore, Chennai.
14. Vivekananda, Swami (1947): *Thoughts on the Gita*. Pp. 80. Advait Ashram, Champavat, Himalayas.
15. Vivekananda, Swami (1976): *Meditation and Its Methods*. Pp. 133. A compilation by Swami Chetananand. Advait Ashram, Champavat, Himalayas.
16. Vivekananda, Swami (1999): *Rajyoga*. Pp. 226. Translation in Hindi by Surya Kant Tripathi 'Nirala' & Guha, D.C.; Ramkrishna Math, Dhantoli, Nagpur.

Know the Vedas At a Glance

—Dr. Raj Kumar, PhD

A clear and concise account on select aspects of the Vedas to gain true knowledge, solve problems of every kind and ensure peace, prosperity and happiness.

The scriptures and classics of a nation are its true heritage, laying a firm foundation for its people to follow. The Vedas are India's and the world's oldest scripture, believed to have been directly revealed by God.

Know the Vedas at a Glance gives a clear and concise account on select aspects of the Vedas, which help dispel ignorance, superstition and false beliefs. The Vedas are replete with guidelines to solve varied problems – social, economic, political, scientific, mental or any other. The message of the Vedas holds relevance for the layman as well as scientists, politicians, educationists, parents and people of every hue. Understanding and following the essence of the Vedas ensures a happy, healthy, peaceful and prosperous life.

Demy Size • Pages: 136
Price: Rs. 80/- • Postage: Rs. 15/-

Divine Message of GOD to MANKIND VEDĀS

–J. M. Mehta

This book, Divine of Message God to Mankind VEDāS is an outcome of a deep study of the main teachings of the four Vedas and broadly contains their essence. The meaning of VEDA is KNOWLEDGE. The teachings of the Vedas represent the original knowledge believed to have been given by God to mankind, at the time of creation. The four Vedas – Rig, Yajur, Sama and Atharva are the fountain head of ancient Indian philosophy, traditions and practices. The Vedās are supposed to contain all true knowledge in seed form. It is enjoined upon mankind to study, understand, develop and propagate this knowledge for individual and universal welfare.

The VEDIC KNOWLEDGE is the key to material as well as spiritual happiness. This small book is a sincere attempt to propagate the main teachings of the Vedas which are DIVINE INSTRUCTIONS for all mankind.

Demy Size • Pages: 168
Price: Rs. 120/- • Postage: Rs. 30/-

VEDA A Way of Life

–Ramanuj Prasad

A treasury of Vedantic teachings

The Veda (Sruti) is the most comprehensive doctrine on religion ever revealed to mankind that answers all man's queries on the here and now and the hereafter. Human objectives can be broadly grouped under four categories: Desire (kama), material gain (artha), religious merits (dharma) and liberation (moksha). The Veda holds the key to fulfil all these aspirations. But the Veda simply reveals the Truth, never pressurising anyone to follow a particular path to self-discovery. Each person is free to choose his own path to discover the Self or God. The Veda acts as a means to the ultimate knowledge that is possible through direct perception.

VEDA: A Way of Life seeks to increase awareness amongst readers about this wonderful treasury of ancient wisdom. Study of this enlightening text will increase values of brotherhood, love and compassion, which are the need of the hour in our troubled times. The Vedic or spiritual way of life promoted by the Veda was later advocated by Lord Krishna through the Bhagavad Gita. This book presents basic tenets of the Veda so that mankind functions according to just eternal laws to ensure universal peace and brotherhood.

Demy Size • Pages: 144
Price: Rs. 96/- • Postage: Rs. 30/-

The LORD'S Song Gita

–Dr. Sant K. Bhatnagar

Gita is the grand repository of spiritual knowledge. The Mahabharata says, Gita comprises all the scriptures as it has emerged directly from God himself. This unique bouquet of heavenly flowers has passed through the hands of millions of readers, but its freshness, beauty and fragrance has not wilted wee-bit, its liveliness has rather increased with every passing moment. It is an unfathomable ocean of knowledge and wisdom; the more we explore the more remains to be explored. Its casts an undying spiritual spell on its votaries. Its keynote is to perform one's duty as duty, and offer all its actions to the lord without attachment to their fruits like a true devotee. This rare bouquet of divine knowledge consists of 700 couplets (shlokas) in Sanskrit language and every shloka radiates divine fragrance and beauty, which is infinite, deathless and imperishable.

Demy Size • Pages: 344
Price: Rs. 160/- • Postage: Rs. 30/-